My Early Life

GRAEME HICK

My Early Life

MACMILLAN
LONDON

First published 1991 by
Macmillan London Limited
Cavaye Place London SW10 9PG
and Basingstoke

Associated companies in Auckland, Delhi, Dublin, Gaborone,
Hamburg, Harare, Hong Kong, Johannesburg, Kuala Lumpur,
Lagos, Manzini, Melbourne, Mexico City, Nairobi, New York,
Singapore and Tokyo

ISBN 0-333-53315-1

A CIP catalogue record for this book is available from the
British Library

Typeset by Macmillan Production Limited

Printed by Billings & Sons Ltd, Worcester, Great Britain

Contents

Acknowledgements

So many people have been influential in my career, but I must start with my parents. They have been totally supportive of me, always there with advice if I asked for it and ready to speak their minds even if I might not like what they had to say. Without their encouragement, I would never have made a success of professional cricket. My sister Sharon has been just as supportive – even though she still thinks I should have had more hidings than I got. Since she married, my brother-in-law Mike's support has been just as loyal.

I would like to thank Rob Altschul and Rex McCullough for their wisdom, enthusiasm and guidance during my schooldays in Zimbabwe. My thanks also to Bill Bourne, the former Warwickshire player, for helping me adjust my technique from schoolboy cricket to the sterner stuff of adult and league cricket. At Worcester, Basil D'Oliveira has been a tremendous help to me – even though I wondered for a long time why he never praised me. I am delighted that he agreed to write the foreword to this book. Mike Vockins, the Worcestershire secretary, has been a tower of strength in sorting out all the necessary paperwork during my qualification period for England: Mike knows that small print isn't my strong point. Duncan Fearnley, the club chairman, Mike Jones, chairman of cricket, our captain Phil Neale and all my team-mates at New Road since 1984 have made me welcome and given me plenty of laughs as well as great moments on the field of play.

Finally, my thanks to Pat Murphy for putting my thoughts and reminiscences down into some sort of order, and for keeping me off the golf course in the process. My swing has suffered, but I hope the end product makes enjoyable reading.

Graeme Hick, November 1990

Introduction by
Basil D'Oliveira, OBE

I shall never forget the first day I saw Graeme Hick. It was early in April 1984 and as the county coach I was supervising Worcestershire's first pre-season net in the usual sub-zero conditions you get in an English spring. I knew that a youngster called Hick was due to report for us that day from Zimbabwe, but I thought little more about it because I had enough on my plate, looking out to see if some of our senior players had wintered too well. We had agreed to take on young Hick largely because of his bowling. Alwyn Pichanik, the President of the Zimbabwe Cricket Union (ZCU) had approached Mike Vockins, asking if the club could take Graeme, whom he rated as 'one of the best batsmen we have produced in Zimbabwe', on a cricketing scholarship for the season. Mike gave a tentative 'yes' but pointed out that the Second XI was well off for young batsmen and if the ZCU had a young off-spinner he might get more opportunities in Second XI cricket. When Pichanik mentioned that Hick also bowled off-spinners the secretary was very interested. 'Right, we'll take him then,' he said. So Graeme came to Worcestershire on the strength of his bowling!

His first net proved he was rather special. When I think about genuinely great batsmen, one of their strokes always stands out. It might be a six off the back foot over cover point by Garry Sobers or a booming on-drive by Ian Botham that sails into the next county. With Graeme Hick, it was a pull in his first net session at New Road. We were practising out in the middle and Paul Pridgeon decided to test out the strapping youngster who had so far looked very impressive driving off the front foot. Paul dug one in short, Graeme swivelled like a flash and the ball went sailing over the bar on the Cathedral side. I wasn't the only one there who whistled softly and looked around, saying, 'Did you see that?' This lad could bat – never mind his off-breaks.

After a quiet start, Graeme really took to life at Worcester that summer. I took him to my old league club, Kidderminster, and he fitted in well there, scoring a stack of runs and joining in with all the fun you have in the bar after a game in English league cricket. By the end of the summer I was desperately worried that another county would have noted his exploits and made an approach to him. Some of our cricket committee were not wholly convinced of Graeme's potential at that stage and I had to convince them he was the genuine article. I assured them he was going to be a great player and they must offer him another contract. I claim no credit for this; anyone who has played the game at the highest level ought to be able to recognise such glittering talent. In the end I got my way, we offered him a contract and the rest is history.

As his coach, I never needed to say much to Graeme about technique; his was beautiful at the age of eighteen, a tribute to the quality of coaching and wickets he had enjoyed in Zimbabwe. I saw my role as a polisher and refiner of his attitude. I'd talk to him about the mental side of the game – how you build an innings, the need to maintain concentration, to forget about the previous ball that almost cleaned you up. He would drink it all in, say very little, narrow his eyes as he memorised it all, go to bed – and next day show how much he had listened to me. All very flattering! I have no time for those players who shoot their mouths off about what they're going to do. That was never Graeme Hick's style. He was quiet and full of common sense in those early days. Nothing has changed in that respect, although success has obviously made him more confident in himself. Graeme has told me in recent years that he was often frustrated that I didn't praise him much, but I think he now realises that I *was* complimenting him. The inferior players – those operating to the extent of their limited abilities – they were the ones who required public praise. All Graeme needed was to be pointed in the right direction.

Of all the great batsmen I have seen, he reminds me of Barry Richards in the amount of time he has to spare when he plays a stroke. He waits for the ball to come to him; lesser batsmen push out at the ball, getting off-balance or playing across the line. Graeme also dismisses the bad ball with more success than any other modern batsman. He has his weaknesses – he is only human. I don't think he plays the cut too well. Sometimes he leans back, gets slightly off-balance and drags the ball on to his stumps. He must work harder at getting his body further over the ball, to cut down hard but safely. Apart from that, he seems to have it all. His attitude to his profession is magnificent, he trains very hard and he has the physical strength to bat for long periods. He loves batting and his temperament for the job is superb. I have no doubt that he is mentally equipped to be a great success in Test cricket. He makes no fuss about his talent, he just gets on with the game. All Graeme needs is an early hundred for England and then we can all settle down and watch him become one of the greats. I am sure he has the necessary killer instinct and his long wait for England qualification has only made him more determined. It is a pity that his bowling has been overshadowed because he has a superb off-spinner's action. He uses his height, bowls line and length and spins it just enough. He will be a very useful option to England if the selectors manage to remember that spin bowlers still exist.

It has given me great pleasure to watch Graeme Hick grow up at New Road. He has shown that a great overseas batsman can also help Counties win the Championship and that it's not always the West Indian fast bowler who is the trump card. Graeme has scored so many runs at speed that he has given us the confidence to attack when we take the field. And his skill at pacing a run chase drives opposing captains to despair.

Graeme is a credit to his family and I am delighted that he and my son Damian have become such firm friends over the years. When he walks out to bat for England, I think only his family will be prouder than me. He hasn't done badly for an off-spinner who can bat a bit!

Basil D'Oliveira

CHAPTER ONE

An Idyllic Childhood

I WAS six years and eight months old when I scored my first hundred. It was for Banket Primary School and my dad still has the scorebook. He tells me I scored twenty-four boundaries out of a total of 102 not out – must have been a hard, bumpy outfield! I remember that the school building was on one side of the ground and that on the other there was a high grass bank; it must have been a big ground for the other small boys to cover. I brought along my little kit bag and wore Dad's old pads, even though they flapped over my knees. We sat beside the scoreboard and, judging by my parents' elation, I had achieved something rather special. I wasn't aware of that at the time because I wasn't following cricket all that closely, and wasn't aware of the importance of such landmarks. I didn't even wear a box – no doubt because there was little to protect! I don't really know how I managed to hit so many boundaries that day because at that age I was pretty frail and of average height; perhaps the bowling wasn't very good, perhaps I struck the ball firmly at the right time. It certainly was a good pitch and that was something I got used to in Zimbabwe. If you wanted to be a batsman, it was a good place to learn.

I didn't get my next hundred till I was eight, but that didn't bother me. Cricket – and all the other sports I played – came naturally and gave me a great deal of fun. It was some time before I took it seriously and it was only after my first year at Worcester (in 1984) that I considered taking it up as a career. Up till then I simply enjoyed the outdoor life in Zimbabwe. That I was good at cricket was very nice but of no great significance to me.

I grew up on a tobacco farm run by my father at Trelawney – about fifty miles from Salisbury, now Harare – and I really can't remember any hard times. Dad has been running the farm for twenty-eight years and there is so much space that we had a clay tennis court built at the back of the house. It was an ideal environment for sports-mad children to grow up in. My sister Sharon and I certainly came into that category. Sharon is four years older than me and, to her delight, she picked up caps in two sports – for the national hockey team and for the basketball side. She never stops telling me that I could only manage to be capped by Zimbabwe in the one sport! Sharon and I have always been close and even now, if she's fussing over me, my brother-in-law, Mike, will say to her, 'Stop worrying about Graeme, he can take care of himself.' Because Sharon and I were so keen on sport, our parents had to divide up their time to come and watch us play. Invariably Mum would watch Sharon and Dad would be there when I played cricket, but whenever possible the whole family would turn up to support whoever was out there playing.

Sport runs in the family. Dad was the country's number-two tennis player at one time and after he had won the necessary competition to qualify him for Junior Wimbledon, he had to decide whether he should go there or enrol for his farming degree. He chose security and although he's never regretted getting his farming qualifications, he must sometimes wonder how he would have done at Wimbledon. I loved playing doubles with him when I was about fifteen; he could manage a court so well, knew all the angles and would carry me. Eventually Sharon and I represented our region at tennis but we were never in Dad's class. He was also a fairly handy cricketer, playing in the first team at school as a wily, slow left-arm spinner and batsman. Although he played for the district side, cricket was mainly a social game for him because of the demands of running the farm. Mum played hockey for the national side for several years and encouraged me to take up that sport when I went to boarding school. I suppose hockey must have helped my cricket progress without my realising it because both sports need a strong sense of hand-to-eye co-ordination. Hockey certainly helped sharpen up my reflexes. I must have been fairly good at the game, because I went on a European tour with the Zimbabwe Junior side at the age of sixteen.

So you get the picture. The four members of the Hick family were very keen on sport with all of them very supportive of each other's efforts. My success in cricket has tended to overshadow the achievements of the other three but just as my parents and Sharon are right behind me in everything I do I am just as loyal to them. We will always be a close-knit family, even though Sharon has now married and presented Mum and Dad with their first grandchild. I don't remember any real upsets in our family (if you ignore the occasional tiffs when I tried to wring Sharon's neck!) and we still miss each other, even if the number of letters from me back to Trelawney has shrunk in recent years. When I went away to boarding school at the age of six, I was lucky because Sharon was already there. On my first night at Banket Primary School, I burst into tears because I felt I was on my own for the first time, but then I ran upstairs and met up with my sister. After a couple of days I was fine and loved being there – especially as I could go home at weekends.

My earliest recollections of cricket are of swinging a Graeme Pollock bat on our front lawn at the age of seven. I remember scraping that bat with a piece of glass to get rid of the linseed oil. I still get a lot of pleasure out of looking after my bats; they have been good friends to me over the years. After that size-three bat, I went to a Gunn and Moore Cannon (size four) and that was the bat I used for my first hundred. I've since realised that it was around this time that I learned the first elements of batting, in particular of playing straight. I was on my own a lot on the farm when I was four or five because Sharon was at school, Dad was at work and Mum was busy. I had to amuse myself or curl up with boredom. I found an old sock, tucked a cricket ball inside it and hung it from a tree. I would then try to hit that sock as often as I could without stopping. Eventually I worked out that if I played the ball straight, it would come back to me at a reasonable angle, instead of waiting for it to fly all over the place from a cross-batted swish. After a while, I got rather efficient at this so I set myself little targets – establishing new records every day for successive hits on the sock. When I came

3

to play competitive cricket I was lucky enough to steer clear of the habit of hitting across the line. Now when I am playing straight, getting a few fours off the front foot past the bowler, I know I am playing well. It is one of the fundamentals of batsmanship and I am lucky I stumbled across it by accident at the age of four.

I had so much energy at that age that I hit upon another way of amusing myself with a cricket bat. I devised a little game that involved a golf ball and our verandah. I would throw the golf ball on to the black polished floor; it would bounce against the verandah wall, come back to me – and I would try to hit it straight back. I didn't hit the ball on the offside, because my parents' bedroom and several windows were on that part of the verandah, so I either played the ball straight back or down in front of me, on to the grass. I'd keep the cycle going for as long as I could, willing myself to beat yesterday's record. So again I was learning to bat properly without realising it. A couple of years later, my dog Womble, a long-haired corgi, performed noble service in helping me beat boredom: he loved chasing after a tennis ball. I would hit it as far as I could and enjoy watching him hare after it. He'd bring it back to me and sit there wagging his tail while I aimed for even greater distance with the next hit. Once he had worked out the location of our swimming-pool, he got a little shrewder; he'd sit there at the top of the pool steps, getting his breath back before returning with a soggy tennis ball! Dad had made a net at the bottom of our garden – with pieces of movable fence surrounding a strip of concrete – and I then taught one of the farm labourers' sons how to bowl. His reward for that was to bowl at me for hours! Eventually the ball was coming quite fast at me and that helped sharpen up my reactions and give me ball sense.

So I was lucky to enjoy an open-air life, to have the time to work at my sport, and to have parents who encouraged me to improve. The climate in Zimbabwe was also perfect for sport, although I couldn't understand it when Mum sometimes refused to let me go out to play in the afternoon heat. When I went to boarding school at the age of six, my luck continued because the sports facilities were very good. Cricket, swimming, tennis, hockey and rugby – you could play all of those. Our master in charge of cricket, Rob Altschul was ideal. He was a very bubbly character who always had a lot of time for us. We all looked forward to our cricket coaching from him, because he made it interesting and fun. I couldn't wait to get through my classes to play cricket. Maybe I had enough talent to have made the grade eventually – but I know that Rob Altschul came along at just the right time for me at that stage of my cricket development. You couldn't help responding to his enthusiasm and obvious love for the game.

Robin Jackman also came along at the right time for me. I was about nine when Robin came to our school to give us coaching lessons. He was filling in his winters in Southern Africa and the experience he had picked up opening the bowling for Surrey was of great benefit to him when he took classes. We were so excited at school when we were told that he was coming; we got working on our equipment, cleaning our boots, whitening our pads to make sure we looked the part. Robin's visits were sponsored by the Dairy Marketing Board and at the end of each session he'd hand out cartons of milk to us from the back of his car. One day I noticed a Gray Nicholls size 5 bat, with the back scooped out, the first of its kind I had seen. I picked it up, admired it and placed it back in the car, only to be told by Robin, 'That's yours.' I was overjoyed. He also gave me a certificate for my performances over the season. That took pride of place in my parents' scrapbook and that bat received the five-star treatment from me; if it's possible to drown a bat in linseed oil, that was the fate of my new Gray Nicholls.

Although I loved playing cricket, I knew very little about the game. I was only vaguely aware of the world's best players – because they were that much nearer, I knew more about those from South Africa. The first cricket book I read was by Tony Greig. It was his account of the 1975 World Cup and it was just right for me, because it contained plenty of glossy pictures, with the players divided into classifications – batsmen, bowlers, wicket-keepers and so on. That made me aware of cricketers beyond South Africa, and Robin Jackman's influence also helped in that direction. Yet I didn't have any great depth of knowledge about the game – I just went out and played it. No day was too long for me, and I was just a typical youngster, who played cricket for fun. It wasn't until a few years later that I was even aware that I was all that good at it.

When I scored my second hundred at the age of eight, my abiding memory was of causing an injury to the scorer, rather than any great sense of achievement. I ended up scoring 132 not out in a total of 162/0 declared, and one of the opposition players was Trevor Penney, who is now on the staff at Warwickshire – like me, he is qualifying as an English player. Trevor's mum was doing the scoring that day, and I remember one of my off-drives hit a boundary stone, shot up and hit her smack on the shin. That must have been a very painful blow. I suppose I must have been timing the ball well to get a four to long-off but the fact that I was obviously hitting with a straight bat didn't mean all that much to me. At eight years of age, you don't have any great ambitions, you just hope it never rains when you're due to play cricket. Dad was very helpful to me at that stage. He realised that you can't be over-technical to someone aged eight or nine, so he didn't overload me with theories. There's no point in going on about keeping the left elbow up to a youngster who just wants to belt the ball. To most of us at that age, batting is a little like baseball, but Dad guided me into certain areas, taught me the basics and the coaches like Rob Altschul and Robin Jackman built on that.

We always played with a hard cricket ball and we were lucky that we played on good, true surfaces. Often fear of a cricket ball stems from playing on poor surfaces where the ball leaps up and smacks you in the face, but we could practise without any such worries. No one bowled all that fast at that age, so I never thought I was in danger when I played forward. The big difference comes a few years later, when teenagers suddenly turn into young men and the ball arrives two yards quicker than you expected. That happened to me, but for now batting was pretty enjoyable. And bowling, I hasten to add. As Dad was a pretty handy slow left-arm spinner, I copied him with my right hand and picked up the basics from him. I knew I had to bowl around off-stump and soon started to turn my off-breaks. I took over a hundred wickets one season for the school when I was nine – I turned it a good deal more than I do now! It was one way to stay in the game once I had finished batting for the day.

I suppose the first hint that I might be more than an ordinary cricketer came when I was ten. I was picked to represent Rhodesian Schools in the annual cricket week in South Africa against their top schoolboys. This was a week of cricket played on a full day schedule sponsored by the Permanent Building Society, known as the Perm Week for teams comprising under-thirteens drawn from all of South Africa's provinces and from Rhodesia. I was the youngest ever from Rhodesia and the youngest cricketer at that Perm Week. We played five days in a row, starting at nine, going on till five o'clock. That was a lot of cricket for our age group and with all our parents turning up to support us it was a great experience, trying to beat the best South African schoolboys. For three successive years I went to that Perm cricket week and in the third year I captained our national team in Cape Town. I remember how much I enjoyed our games in those cricket weeks: I got a few runs, but for some reason I remember the wickets I took more clearly. I took 8/25 one day against Griqualand West, but we still lost! A few years later, politics had entered the fray and, with President Mugabe taking over the direction of Zimbabwe, all sporting links with South Africa were discouraged.

When I was picked for the Fawns under-fifteen side to go to South Africa for the cricket week, our team missed out on the trip at the very last minute – we were just getting on to the coach in Harare when we were told the visit had been cancelled. So I missed out on the Nuffield Week as well due to politics – that's for under-eighteens and it would have been a great test of our standard. Traditionally if you perform well in the Nuffield Week, you can go straight into a Currie Cup side and be playing first-class cricket within a few weeks. But it was not to be. A great pity, because getting involved in such hard competition for five days in a row when you are just ten is a great way to toughen you up and develop your competitive instinct.

Despite the open-air life that the Hick family led, I was a pretty sickly child till I was about twelve. I was six weeks premature at birth and went straight into an incubator. I had a weak chest for quite a few years and suffered every winter, shovelling down the vitamin C whenever I could. It took me a long time to settle down to consistent good health and I was always a stringbean at school, with nothing on me. We are a tall family (at six feet one, Mum is an inch taller than Dad), but I didn't shoot up until I was about fifteen. I dreaded winters. After a hot day in the sun, Mum would insist I put on a jumper around 4.30, so I wouldn't catch cold. Mind you, Zimbabwe's definition of winter is somewhat different to England's: on the farm, winter came when it was overcast and about seventy degrees! When I was seven and a boarder at school, several times I caught pneumonia and shortly afterwards, when my resistance was low, I developed asthma. For years afterwards, I used to dread it when Dad lit up his pipe. One day he managed to lose it and it then dawned on him what a disgusting habit it was. He's never smoked it since, with the result that his son no longer suffers from chest complaints.

More seriously, I contracted meningitis when I was thirteen and for months after that I felt totally drained. At the start, the doctors didn't know whether it was malaria, meningitis or cerebral malaria; our family knew of a chap who had just died of cerebral malaria and for a couple of days that was a distinct possibility. I needed a pint of water to wash down pills the size of golf balls and they stuck huge needles in me when they gave me lumbar punctures. When one of the needles came out, it caught one of my nerves and I sat bolt upright. I was then advised to play as much sport as possible to strengthen my leg, and that was no hardship! Ever since then, if I have been on my feet for a long period, I get a tingling feeling in my left leg. Since I took up aerobics to develop extra flexibility, it's decreased but it's still there as a reminder of meningitis. I was so weak when I got out of hospital that I fell in the bath one night as I leaned forward to adjust the taps. Sport was out for at least six months and the only consolation for Mum was that I had to concentrate on my classwork – that was never my strong point, but I did improve for a short period!

So I wasn't exactly an impressive physical specimen when I was at Prince Edward's High School, Harare, at the age of thirteen, though I was lucky that I had been toughened up at primary school. There, right from the start, the school cap had to be worn at all times, ties done up to the neck, our socks had to have garters and we had to doff our caps to the teachers every time we passed by. From the age of six, we were caned if we'd done anything wrong and it became a fact of life that you'd get a beating two or three times a week. You'd bathe your backside in methylated spirits to toughen you up for the cane.

So I knew what to expect by the time I got to Prince Edward's. It was all to do with testing your mettle, to see if you could come through the various physical and mental tests. In the rugby season, I had to look after the kit of one of the seniors. Unfortunately he was the hooker in the side and as he spent a lot of time on the ground his jersey was always very dirty. I used to wash it three times a week with a scrubbing brush, standing in the shower, working away at it till it was spotless. The socks were a problem because the white part would run into the red and become pink. That had to be sorted out before the next match day, or else my reward was a beating. For two years, I had to polish the shoes of a senior every morning, make his bed, carry his case to school and lay out his fresh clothes in the evening.

It may sound absurd to say so, but all this was good for me because it taught me respect for my elders. If someone was older – even if only by a couple of years – he had to be respected. Now and then the seniors used to beat us with a track shoe just because they were bored and fancied a half-hour's distraction. You'd run the gauntlet of shoes, tennis balls and pillows being thrown at you as you scampered over and under the beds. It wasn't personal, just tradition. If a senior wanted some food or a drink from the tuckshop, he would call on any junior and send him off on the errand and invariably he'd find himself going back and forwards for half an hour, serving a growing band of seniors. And you had to remember to bring back the right change! One of the chaps in our year was taken away from the school by his parents once they found out about the various rituals, but he was unlucky because he was unathletic and a bit podgy, so the seniors picked on him. He didn't want to leave, though.

The vital thing was not to show pain. Many times I'd go into the dormitory and wish I was anywhere else but Prince Edward's, but that soon passed. It could easily have got out of hand, but the masters knew exactly what was going on and I think the seniors stayed on the right side of testing us out, rather than being cruel. I think I got away with it fairly lightly because I was good at sport – although I offer a different story when I meet up with my old schoolmates! I believe boarding school helped me. It's a process of life I had to go through and I think it has helped me stand on my own two feet, especially when I first came over to Worcester and began a career thousands of miles from home, feeling lonely. I think boarding school also taught me manners, and today, when I see English schoolboys thrusting their autograph books in my face and using bad language in front of adults, I feel they could do with a few terms at Prince Edward's. In my first fortnight there, I had no idea why I had to memorise the names of all those in the first team for rugby and cricket, and of all the prefects. I just did it, without realising that we were being pushed on, making us more disciplined. Everyone who has been to Prince Edward's is proud of the fact, so the pride and tradition must have its roots in coming through little tests like memorising sportsmen's names.

Academic achievements cut little ice at Prince Edward's, which is just as well since I never impressed anyone in that department of life. For me and many others, sport was the main attraction, with classwork a disagreeable pastime till we could get out on to the playing fields again. The school has a great sporting tradition – the golfers, Nicky Price and Mark McNulty are old boys, as are many former Springbok rugby players. The sporting facilities were magnificent and there was a subtle way of making you aim high for honours. If you had played for the first team at rugby or cricket, you were allowed to walk across a certain playing field, otherwise you had to walk all the way round it. That was a good incentive to shine and so was our colours blazer. All the top boys had a colours blazer for being in a first team and you aimed for that. I played in the under-thirteens first team at rugby, but soon concentrated on hockey because I liked going on death-or-glory runs with a massive stick, trying to whack the ball in from an impossible angle.

After we had played hockey on the Saturday morning, we had to attend the first-team rugby game. It was compulsory – your name was ticked off – so eight hundred of us would sit there, looking at the opposition supporters, chanting our war-cry. Even if it was hot, we had to wear tie, blazer and boater – and at the end of our war-cry, we'd throw our boaters in the air, before racing to retrieve it. All this may sound very juvenile, but I believe it gave me a respect for team sports and for my colleagues in that team. I've never been obviously gritty – I don't go in for clenched fists and punching the air at triumphant moments – but I do think I am mentally tough in a quiet sort of a way. The best thing I learned from my sport at boarding school was a feeling of togetherness on the field, and that's why I like team sports so much. It's a great feeling to be part of a successful team, and in recent years it has given me great satisfaction to have played a part in Worcestershire's capture of so many trophies.

Prince Edward's also drummed into me the importance of playing to win. The facilities on offer for sports-mad boys were so good that you wanted to excel. So when I tried running and various field events I eventually settled on those I could win. I broke the school's record for pole vault and the discus, and I can't deny that was a good feeling. If you were outstanding at sport at that school, you were somebody in the eyes of your peers. Even with the social games like cards, dominoes or charades I want to win – though not Trivial Pursuit: I can't answer those difficult questions! Even in mixed doubles at tennis, I like to nip in with a killing volley if I feel we might be losing. I'll try to do it without any fuss; I don't see why you have to shout it from the rooftops that you're trying hard to win, but I don't see any fun in losing if you can help it.

By the time I got to Prince Edward's, I had a reasonable name as a cricketer, even though I had only played for Banket Primary School and then for Rhodesian Schools in South Africa. Again I was lucky. The master who took the under-fourteens for cricket was a major influence on that stage of my career. Rex McCullough was a great character; at that time he was in his mid-fifties, yet he still looked very smart at the nets, with all the right cricket gear on, including white socks kept up by garters. He'd never let you wear any old white shirt – it had to be a proper cricket one, with long sleeves, and you had to wear the school cap and belt. If you didn't turn up properly dressed or messed around in the nets, he'd kick you out of the session. Rex had a great knowledge of the game and he was highly respected – old boys of the school were always turning up to see him when he was taking us in the nets, and we could see why. He made sure we practised hard; no one was allowed to slog, otherwise they were sent packing. He was happy for you to go down the wicket and hit over the top, but no slogging. Some days he'd bring a box of brand-new cricket balls and he'd warn us that anyone who dropped a catch in fielding practice was finished for the day. Sure enough, the first to do so was sent away and although we all laughed at the unlucky boy, it made us concentrate even harder. Rex refused to take the first team for practice, because he felt that thirteen to fourteen was the best age to guide the boys. So he came at just the right time for me. Early on I scored a hundred for the Under-Thirteen A side and he told me that I wouldn't be playing for them again. He told me to pick up my kit and go and join the Under-Fourteen A team in their nets. He used to give a bat to anyone who scored a hundred, and after my promotion I got seven centuries that school season, averaging 216, and scoring just over a thousand runs. I never got a bat off him, though! I did get a long cricket bag, with my name and that of my school written along the side, so I can't complain.

In case anyone thinks that I was treated differently from the others because I was the star player, I can prove that wasn't so. Every Sunday in those days, it was my job to get all the cricket results from all the houses at the school, from Under-Thirteen to Under-Eighteen. I then had to write them all down and take them to the headmaster's office. He would then read them out at assembly on Monday morning. Even at the age of thirteen, I knew very little about the way cricket was discussed or reported on; I didn't know about seven-wicket wins, I just thought you subtracted one score from the other. So I would tell the headmaster that a team that scored 58 for 3 in reply to 56 all out had won by two runs! One day, I could see that the headmaster was very puzzled by my scoring system and sure enough he asked 'the young gentleman who has collected these scores' to wait behind and see him. He then put me right about how teams win cricket matches in different ways.

So I was not part of any star system at Prince Edward's just because I got more runs than the others. The idea of team spirit was far too important for any individual to get big ideas, and that should always be the case. I later realised that Rex McCullough was keeping a close eye on my progress and keeping my parents informed, but I knew nothing of that, thankfully. I was enjoying life there too much to be singled out for special attention. One thing I am proud of, though: no cricket team that I played in at Prince Edward's ever lost a game. That still means more to me than averaging 216 at the age of thirteen.

CHAPTER TWO

The First Big Leap

T HE first major progression in my career came when I started to play adult cricket at the age of fifteen. Of course, I didn't know it at the time – for me, it was just a case of spending Sundays playing for Old Hararians after turning out for my school the day before. Old Hararians was basically an extension of Prince Edward's and it seemed the most natural thing to do to play for them on a Sunday. They'd had some great years under Mike Procter and Jackie du Preez (who also played for South Africa) but by the time I came along the club was going through a bad patch and had ended up in the Second Division of the local league. So they decided to blood the youngsters – and once again I was lucky enough to be in the right place at the right time. Soon I was playing league cricket at the age of fourteen, and that lasted for the next three years – schools cricket on the Saturday, then up against the adults over sixty overs a side the next day.

People often ask me why I've done so well at cricket and I think some of it has to do with moving up a grade at the right moment. From schools cricket onwards, things seem to have happened to me, whereby through no choice of my own I'd be put up to face a higher standard, just when I needed an extra test. It has happened all the way through my career so far, and I just hope that if I am selected for England, I don't find the gulf too great. Mind you, there was nothing unusual about playing in the league while so young in Zimbabwe. In England it's considered special if you get into league cricket at seventeen or eighteen, whereas a combination of sunshine, good wickets and sound coaching at school seemed to mature young cricketers that much earlier in my time with Old Hararians. The standard of cricket was just as good as in the Birmingham League in my opinion.

My schoolboy reputation meant nothing when I started playing for Old Hararians. The older players just regarded me as a team-mate and relied on me to swim rather than sink. In my first league game for them, I got 52 in an opening stand of just over 200 and soon I settled in at number three. We won the Second Division championship and then the Knockout Cup the following year. It was a great time to be part of a young, developing side and we had no inhibitions because we were playing well and were encouraged to approach the game positively. Playing against adults was good for me, because they hit the ball that little bit harder and the ball was delivered a good deal faster. Just because you were fifteen didn't mean the fast bowlers dropped their pace – you had to play on their terms. It was good for my development. Socially as well – after the game the younger ones would sit around, listening to the senior players telling yarns over a beer. Soon I graduated to a glass or two myself! One night, when I was at the stage of discovering girls, I had gone on to a disco in Harare after playing for the school, even though I was due to play in the league the next day. My parents were staying with me in town that weekend and when I crept in at three o'clock in the morning, my mother was waiting for me just as the key went into the front-door lock. 'Where have you been till this time? You've got a big game in a few hours – get to bed!' she hissed at me. I shot upstairs, managed to grab a few hours' sleep, dashed down to the ground at nine o'clock – and scored a hundred. That let me off the hook!

Soon life for me revolved around the Old Hararians Sports Club at the weekend, whatever the season. The ground was only five minutes' walk from school, so after hockey or cricket for the school on Saturday, I'd play both for the club side on the Sundays. I'm sure the fact that I played a lot of other sports helped my fielding when I started to play league cricket. That is one area where schoolboys can be caught out when playing with adults because the ball can come screaming at you with terrific power. But hockey in particular helped sharpen up my reflexes and, as I've always had big hands, fielding at a higher level came fairly easy to me. I was taught the basics of fielding early on and I've been happy to field anywhere. It gives you an added interest in the game. As a batsman, I soon realised that one of the major differences between schools and league cricket was that on a Sunday I wasn't getting two balls an over that could be put away for four. The bowlers were much more accurate, and the fielding captain was more alert to tactical possibilities, like getting me off the strike by giving me a single or setting a particular field to different batsmen. There was very little of that in schools cricket, where my ability to put away the bad ball helped me pile up big scores. Against the adults, I had to work harder for my runs and that was good for me.

My first lesson in the difference in pace came when I was fifteen. I was taking part in a trial for the Zimbabwe Under-Nineteen side to face English Schools who were touring at the time. The opposition had a big nineteen-year-old who was distinctly fast. While sitting with my pads on, I had watched him closely and came to the conclusion that not only was he distinctly swift, he was also dangerous. He lacked control, so there was every chance that he would send down an unintentional beamer while trying for the fast yorker. When I went in to bat, I was a little uptight. The first ball from him was flicked off my toes to the midwicket boundary and then, much to my relief, he was taken off. Perhaps the captain thought that that first scoring shot suggested I might take the guy apart, but I certainly didn't feel comfortable and was very happy to see him take his sweater. So I got away with that one, but things were very different when I faced Bill Bourne in the nets at school a year later.

Bill had been a medium-pace bowler with Warwickshire a few years earlier, but to me he was like a genuine quickie. He had come over to coach at Zimbabwean schools, trying to help the Zimbabwe Cricket Union to raise standards, and he certainly helped improve my batting. In just three balls, he bowled me twice with yorkers. He was yards quicker than anything I'd yet faced. Bill told me that I'd get by in schools cricket with my bat in the crease waiting for the bowler, but that I should think about having my bat raised when I played against adults because of the contrast in pace. Certainly he was through me with my bat still on the floor, so I followed his advice. I stood there, bat raised, and it felt right; it also gave me vital moments to get at the faster ball. Ever since then, I have stood with my bat raised and, although some pundits deplore that technique, I have to say that it suits me. Sometimes I will play with the bat at my feet in the nets, as I just push at the ball and work at my timing, but I want to be comfortable at the crease and it feels right with my bat just above the stumps while waiting for the bowler. Many said that we should all follow the lead of the Australians who batted so well in England in 1989, because they were technically correct and successful – but I feel a batsman has to use the method which suits him best. It suits Steve Waugh to stand at the crease with his bat at his feet, but I am much taller than he is and I need to play upright. If you are tall, I believe you should stand up and use your height to your advantage. I rarely get yorked with my method, so there must be some reliability in my approach. I tend to think that a still head which enables you to watch the ball closely is more important than where the bat is positioned as the bowler is about to deliver.

I'm often asked when I developed the tendency to score big hundreds, to go on past the three-figure mark, refusing to play loosely and give my wicket away. As far as I can remember I always had that desire, as long as it didn't conflict with the interests of the side. At school and club cricket level, there are many players who are quite happy to reach a particular landmark and give their wicket away after that, but I never really saw the point in that. Obviously you loosen up a little as your innings grows, but I didn't believe in throwing the bat at the ball without any idea. I'll always try to quicken the scoring rate – especially if my team needs that – but there's a big difference between playing confidently and slogging. I'll take risks for the good of the side, but if you start to panic at the crease you lose control and the bowlers are halfway there. When I was turning out for Old Hararians, nothing gave me greater pleasure than batting, though I really enjoyed bowling my off-breaks (and I soon realised that you don't get away with loose deliveries against league batsmen). We had a maximum of sixty overs and I was always encouraged to play properly. The older players in the side supported me all the way and I never felt anyone was complaining behind my back that I was occupying the crease for far too long, denying a chance to others. So I'd keep going on good wickets, learning all the time, and doing my best for the side.

League cricket tightened up my game sufficiently to get me into the Zimbabwe Schools side that faced English Schools on a short tour in 1982. I was sixteen and some of the players on both sides were nearly nineteen, but I was pleased with my efforts. They were a strong outfit – including John Stephenson, Steven Goldsmith, Graham Rose and Gary Palmer, all of whom eventually played county cricket. We were outplayed, but it was another great experience for me, taking on older players and getting top score in both internationals at Bulawayo and Harare. I learned later that those English players said some nice things about me and I did feel I had performed satisfactorily. I was scoring a lot of runs in the league at the time, and I'm sure the confidence I brought into the internationals stemmed from that.

A couple of months later, I was less successful on my next step up the ladder. The Young Australians had come to Zimbabwe and I was picked to play against them for Zimbabwe Colts. The fact that the game was played at my local club, the Harare Sports Club, didn't relax me all that much because I just couldn't cope with the speed of Mike Whitney. Whitney played against England in 1981 and for most of the 1980s he took a fair amount of wickets for New South Wales as a reliable seam bowler of fast–medium pace, never more than that. To me, at sixteen years of age, he was like greased lightning. I went in first wicket down, with the total on 4, and I wore all the protective equipment I could find. I hadn't worn a helmet or visor before, but I was glad I'd borrowed one from a schoolmate. The first ball I faced was the last of the over from him and all I saw was the ball leaving his hand – nothing more. I thrust out my pad in desperation, and somehow the ball hit my bat at least three yards earlier than I had expected. The ball went straight back to the bowler and I breathed again. I didn't last very long – Whitney had me caught at slip for a duck. I was nervous and felt out of my depth for the first time in cricket. There was nothing wrong with the pitch, but they still bowled us out for 43, after we were 7 for 5 at one stage. Whitney and Rod McCurdy were just too sharp for us.

That was a strong Australian team, with players like Greg Ritchie, Dirk Welham, David Boon, Robbie Kerr and Wayne Phillips: a day or two later, they beat the senior Zimbabwe side by an innings. I didn't play against them for the rest of that tour, which suited me fine! That experience just underlined the vast gulf that existed between Test players and those who play keen club cricket at weekends in Harare. As someone still playing for his school on a Saturday, it was an even bigger shock.

So I went back to the league without giving a thought to any further appearances for Zimbabwe. If I had been asked, I would have said that I was too young and raw and needed toughening up against better opposition. I wasn't particularly depressed, though, because cricket was still just fun. Within a few weeks, my cricket education was to be greatly advanced.

CHAPTER THREE

The Schoolboy International

I N 1983, my last year at school, I was part of the greatest moment yet in the history of Zimbabwe cricket. The World Cup staged in England was the first time our cricket had been taken seriously in other parts of the world and, although my role in that was insignificant, it was a great experience for a shy schoolboy to be there, taking it all in. I was on that trip purely to gain experience: my runs in league cricket must have suggested I had some promise but my nought against Young Australia had shown there was no point in rushing me too quickly. So I was sent as junior pro and 'baggage man' and allowed to play a few friendlies on the tour.

I was perfectly happy not to play in any of the World Cup games for the simple reason that I knew I would be out of my depth. I hadn't forgotten those few balls from Mike Whitney a few months earlier and I knew that the West Indies had bowlers who were much quicker than him: how could I expect to see, never mind play, anything bowled by Michael Holding, Malcolm Marshall or Joel Garner? Before each World Cup match, we'd gather for a team meeting the night before and I'd sit there, thinking, 'Please don't pick me, they're too quick for me.' I wasn't used to such negative thoughts – most of my cricket up till then had gone so well – but I knew I'd be swept away. I was content to field as a substitute and just soak it all up.

A visit to Buckingham Palace the day before the tournament started was a highlight, but it also brought me face to face with my naivety. All the teams gathered in a massive room at the Palace to be presented to the Queen and Prince Philip. I came up against this huge man wearing a maroon blazer; I couldn't see past him, he was so massive. I looked up and recognised him as Joel Garner. I couldn't believe that somebody so tall could be so athletic and fast – at that moment I felt tremendous relief that I was not going to have to bat against him, that I was only in England for the experience.

Then we all lined up for the royal introduction. I kept memorising what the public relations man had told us – 'Your Majesty' when addressing the Queen and 'Your Royal Highness' for Prince Philip. When I was finally presented to them, I had a mental block, forgot everything I'd been told, mumbled 'Hi' and walked off. After that, the younger and less sophisticated members of our team stuck together during the reception, getting the champagne down our necks as the waiters came round with their silver trays. Even more pleasant from my point of view was the sight of cashews in little bowls. I have always loved cashews – they are difficult to get in Zimbabwe – and I couldn't resist helping myself to fistfuls of them, and putting them in my blazer pocket in case the waiter didn't come back again with the tray. But he did – and I just couldn't refuse them. I've never eaten so many in my life. All the while the Queen was very graciously walking around the room, talking to all the players, but as soon as we younger players saw that she was coming near us, we would slide over to the other side of the room. We weren't being rude, it was just that we knew we would be too tongue-tied to think of anything to say to her and we didn't want to let the side down.

Although I already knew most of our team before we came to England (many of us were based in Harare), I kept myself very much to myself on that first tour. I tended to clam up in company or in places I didn't know and didn't fancy going out to pubs or clubs, like the other guys. I was lonely a lot of the time and wrote a lot of letters home to my parents. I wasn't unhappy – it was all a learning process – but I had this strange negative feeling about England. I'd got this idea in my head that it was a country full of drug addicts and muggers and I had no intention of going out of my hotel unless I had to. Apart from attending official functions with the rest of the team, I went to a pub only once on that trip. Once I went to a club with some of the guys in Nottingham, but I didn't like the noise and thought that criminals were lurking nearby, waiting to mug me or try to force drugs on me. It sounds ridiculous, I know, but I had led a very sheltered life, revolving around sport, the farm, school and family, and the few snippets I had read about England had worried me. I was perfectly happy to go back to the hotel after cricket, put my feet up and watch television in my room. At that time television in Zimbabwe consisted of one black-and-white channel and I was fascinated by the choice of four TV channels in colour. I also got stuck into Mars bars, McDonald's burgers and Kentucky Fried Chicken, none of which were available back home.

So I was in my element in my hotel room; why did I need clubs or pubs? I also saved a lot of money, because I didn't blow my daily allowance like a lot of the others. By the end of the tour, I had about a thousand pounds to spend in London and I blew it on some great shopping sprees. One day I came back to the hotel weighed down with tracksuits, training shoes and sweatshirts, just as the others were getting out of bed. They couldn't work out where I had got it all from until I told them, 'I didn't drink my money away like you lot!' When I got back home, Mum took a photo of me with all my sports gear laid out – with twelve sets of shoes, my sponsorship gear from Gunn and Moore, and all the stuff I had bought in London, I had enough to open a sports shop. In one of those London sports shops, I saw Bjorn Borg (chased by autograph hunters) promoting his own sportswear, and I also went to Wimbledon to watch Martina Navratilova and Kevin Curren on the Centre Court. I did the tourist bit one day in London – Hyde Park Corner, St Paul's Cathedral, the Houses of Parliament, the full works – and took enough photographs to keep my family happy.

The cricket was pretty interesting as well. It was a great day for us all when Zimbabwe beat Australia in our first game, at Trent Bridge. That day we really played above ourselves while the Aussies were a little below par, but it was still a great achievement to beat them, and people sat up and took notice of us. We fielded superbly, spending a lot of time in practice. We also knew how to field: many professional cricketers don't seem to know how to commit themselves to a fifty/fifty ball, to dive properly. Many seem to dive over the ball, or go for it when the ball has gone past. There's an art in timing the dive, spreading yourself a long way and keeping your eyes on the ball, and that Zimbabwe side was very good at it. Perhaps we were also more committed early in that World Cup than the other, more experienced sides. We had never played Test cricket – apart from John Traicos with South Africa – and it was the highlight of our careers to be up against so many world-class players.

Many of our players had had experience of first-class cricket, so the team talks were conducted properly. We knew the opposition were an unknown quantity to us, that there was no point dwelling on their obvious talent, so we concentrated on getting the best out of ourselves. That meant bowling tightly, fielding well and concentrating hard when we batted. Many of our team had experience of English conditions, both from playing in the leagues and from winning the ICC (International Cricket Conference) Trophy the year before, so we weren't exactly a pushover, and some sides perhaps relaxed a little against us.

We had India in all sorts of trouble at Tunbridge Wells. They were 17 for 5 and then Kapil Dev came in to play an astonishing innings of 175 not out. Grant Paterson almost caught him; indeed, he actually caught him at long on, but ran into the boundary boards and split his finger. So I came on as substitute fielder and had a first-hand view of Kapil's amazing knock. I was dying for him to hit one up in the air so I could catch him, but I only fielded a few. I got to know Kapil when I joined Worcestershire and he told me that he just chanced his arm that day and got lucky. He said he kept swinging the bat and hoping that nothing would go to hand, and apart from a couple that stayed a long time in the air, he kept hitting the ball cleanly. We felt we'd bowled really well, but it was one of those knocks when you just have to admire his confidence and applaud the way he pulled India around.

Yet we weren't far off winning, despite Kapil's great knock. Jack

Heron and Robin Brown were both run out and Kevin Curran hit one to extra cover when he was going really well and the Indians were getting worried. We lost by only 31 runs but, with more experience of this type of situation, I am sure we would have got the runs. We just needed a couple of good individual performances and some cool heads and we would have got home. That would have been our second win and we might just have sneaked into the semi-finals.

Exactly a week later, India won the World Cup, so that just shows how important that innings by Kapil was to his side. He gave them the confidence to go on and beat England and then, in the final, the West Indies in a major upset. We were lucky enough to stay on to watch the final and it was fascinating to see the confidence surge through the Indians as the favourites kept getting out. The West Indies only needed 180-odd to win, yet if they had been set around 250 they would have stood a better chance. They got bogged down on a slow wicket and instead of playing their natural game, they became too negative and didn't break free of the pressure the Indians started to exert on them. The turning-point was Kapil's marvellous catch to get rid of Viv Richards. It was almost like a setpiece in American football, whereby Viv seemed to tell Kapil where he was going to hit the ball; it was as if Kapil set off before the ball was on Viv, giving him precious time to get to the mishit hook.

At that stage in my cricket career, I thought the best batsmen got most of the runs and the bulk of the wickets would fall to the quickest bowlers, but that Lord's final made me realise that cricket is more complex than that. On slow pitches, it's sometimes the nudgers and deflectors who are more valuable batsmen and the bowlers who can drop the ball on line and length, frustrating the batsmen, who win matches. I wasn't aware that so many pitches in England were slow, with the result that it can be difficult to score off certain bowlers. India had a few of them on hand that day and the West Indies batsmen kept getting themselves out. The bowlers were allowed to put the ball on the spot and the pressure just mounted on Viv Richards and the others. That was a lesson I learned over and over again when I came to play in England. Not every country had wickets like those in Zimbabwe.

So that tour to England helped me a lot as a cricketer, even though the nearest I got to the big time was as a substitute fielder. I fielded throughout the West Indies innings at Edgbaston, when Haynes and Bacchus put on 170-odd to win by ten wickets; I was at third man and mid-on, making routine throws into the wicket-keeper as they stole singles. The winning hit went past me at mid-on and as I turned to chase the ball I saw swarms of West Indian supporters coming towards me, heading for their two batsmen; I did a sharp detour, left the ball to the supporters and legged it back to the pavilion! It was a big jump for us to play against a side like the West Indies, but I think we all learned a lot from it. We now knew more about the place to bowl in limited-overs matches and how to take singles to disrupt the field. It was to be another couple of months before the lessons of that tour really sank into me, when I was back in Zimbabwe, telling my family and friends about everything I had seen. For me it had been a case of attending team meetings, helping with practice on the morning of a match, watching the play from the dressing room and occasionally standing in as a fielder. I wasn't frustrated – I did get a few knocks in friendlies – and I was more than happy not to come up against the likes of Lillee, Thomson, Hogg and the West Indies fast bowlers. I would have liked a gentler attack – like India's or Sri Lanka's – but I was content just to watch the play and support the team.

I think Zimbabwe came out of that 1983 tour with a good reputation. Duncan Fletcher was a very good captain, able to motivate the players, kick a few backsides if necessary and pull the team along with him. Kevin Curran showed the all-round talent that brought him to Gloucestershire, David Houghton was a quality wicket-keeper/batsman and John Traicos bowled his off-breaks very effectively. Unfortunately, two of our best batsmen – Andy Pycroft and Jack Heron – kept running each other out at crucial times; if they had sorted out their calling, the side would have fared even better. Yet we didn't disgrace ourselves. Several of our players had been toughened up by Currie Cup cricket in previous years and, with just a little more experience of combating pressure in big games, we would have done even better.

A few months after that World Cup tour, I left school. After yet another miserable failure at passing my 'O' Levels, I was allowed to give up the academic pretence and settle down to playing league cricket and going on tours with the senior Zimbabwe side. Before the year was out, I had been to Zambia and Sri Lanka, very much the junior still, but loving the travelling, wielding the camera whenever I could, and learning more about cricket.

The Zambian trip in September involved a triangular tournament (the other teams were Kenya and an East African XI), and although the cricket wasn't very exciting – we were too good – there were some interesting moments. While walking round the ground up in the Copperbelt one day, I saw our pavilion going up in smoke after a stray cigarette had set fire to the thatched roof – the fact that the fire engine was there within a minute of the alarm being raised made me wonder if it was a regular occurrence! On one of our internal flights in Zambia, we had to use the kind of plane you see in the old movies – with the propellers being cranked up on the ground and very cramped inside. That was a hairy flight. I was still baggage boy on that tour, even though I was our most successful bowler, but I had no problems about that. As the youngest member of the squad, I had to get used to adult humour and being the butt of most practical jokes. A plastic snake that was almost too realistic made me jump out of my skin one day when I was told to go to one of the player's cases to get out some cricket balls. It was all in good fun and there was no point in taking offence. I enjoyed being in the company of adults and I think it helped me grow up.

Our tour to Sri Lanka was an altogether different experience. We had three weeks of rain and hardly played, but when we did get on the field at Colombo, up in the tea-plantation area, the game was soon called off and our bus was stoned. It wasn't our fault, since the outfield was saturated, but after three hours of trying to play it became a farce. The local officials told us to make our way stealthily out of the pavilion and not to give any clue that the game had been abandoned: the announcement over the PA system would be delayed until we were in the coach. Some of the more volatile members of the crowd got wind of this and surrounded our coach, rocking it to and fro, and throwing bricks at us. In the end our manager shouted, 'Just drive!' and we roared off. How we escaped serious injury I shall never know.

By the end of 1983, I could look back on a significant year. I had been to England, Zambia and Sri Lanka – all thanks to cricket. Although I still saw it as an adventure, I hadn't disgraced myself. I made my first-class debut in October, against the Young West Indians, in Harare at the age of seventeen years and five months. I batted at number seven – keeping the youngster away from the firing line – and when I went out to face Courtney Walsh and George Ferris, I was wearing every piece of armour-plating I could lay my hands on. I managed to glide them away for several fours in my 28 not out before the declaration came, and I enjoyed the experience. It was hard coming to terms with the speed of their bowlers and, in one of the limited-overs games, I closed my eyes to one delivery off Rod Estwick and just swung hopefully at it. As I opened my eyes, I saw the ball soaring over midwicket, a shot that wasn't exactly from the textbook! That was the first time I had tried the pull shot in any class of cricket; before, there wasn't much need because I could get on to the front foot against most of the bowlers in Zimbabwe. The fast, short stuff only really came at me when the Australians or West Indians were touring. At seventeen, I was beginning to realise that batting wasn't just a case of dismissing well-pitched-up balls for four.

We did well against that young West Indian side, despite their quick bowlers. Their support bowling was thin, while our senior batsmen played very well; Peter Rawson, our swing bowler, had an excellent series and John Traicos gave nothing away with his off-spin. Again we fielded marvellously, especially in the one-day games. We were just as dominant in the one-day matches a few months later against the Young Indians. They brought a side over that was full of current Test players or those soon to make a mark in Test cricket – Shastri, Srikkanth, Azharuddin, Prabhakar and Maninder Singh – but we more than held our own against them. I found myself in at number three for that series, a pleasant prospect compared to facing the West Indians from that position. I got a few runs in the one-dayers, but I remember vividly being outwitted by their slow left-armer, Maninder Singh. He did me with his arm ball as I tried to cut one off the middle stump; he lined me up pretty well, bowled it a little quicker and down went my middle stump. I was learning that the better bowlers were more adaptable than the club ones that I was playing against.

So I was still finding my feet in international cricket when that season ended. That senior Zimbabwe side was a handy outfit at that time, with a lot of experience and a great team spirit, so it was an ideal environment in which to bring on a promising schoolboy like me. Nothing remarkable was expected of me, I knew I was there to learn, and it was rewarding to go up a few gears and play against Test cricketers. Unknown to me, steps were being taken to further my cricket education. Alwyn Pichanick, the president of the Zimbabwe Cricket Union, approached my parents and suggested that I should go to England on a cricket scholarship to get experience. They talked about sending me to Lord's for a place on the MCC Groundstaff, but they felt I wouldn't play enough cricket, that I'd spend too much time bowling in the nets, helping clean up the ground or selling scorecards on matchdays.

By this time, I was in on the discussions and agreed with them: if I was going to England, I wanted to play as much cricket as I could. They talked about sending me to Leicestershire, and that appealed because I vaguely knew Paddy Clift and Brian Davison from their days in Zimbabwe. Unfortunately Leicestershire already had Mike Haysman on a scholarship, and with a large staff there was no room for me. When the ZCU applied to the Test and County Cricket Board on my behalf, they suggested going to Worcestershire. I recalled sitting in the members' bar at Worcester, watching the West Indies beating Zimbabwe the previous year, and I was quite happy about that. At least I wouldn't be going somewhere that was totally foreign to me – I could picture the ground and I remembered it was pretty. I was still concerned about going to a place where I knew no one, and I hadn't got over my obsession with crime in England, but my parents and Alwyn Pichanick seemed to think it would be good for me.

There were few professional options for me in Zimbabwe. I never really fancied farming – if Dad had owned Trelawney Estate it would have been different, and it would have been nice to keep it in the family, but he was just the farm manager. Besides I would have had to pass exams for that, and I hadn't really distinguished myself in that direction at school. After two stabs at my 'O' Levels, I had ended up with the grand total of four – English Language and Literature, Maths and Geography. That didn't exactly equip me for the job I had really fancied – as a vet. I had always loved animals (we usually had about six pets around the farm) and I would have liked caring for them, but you have to be fairly good at academic work to qualify. So there weren't many alternatives to keep me occupied in the spring of 1984. I talked the situation over with Mum and Dad and they suggested I should give cricket a go for one summer over in Worcester, and then think about another career. For the moment, I'd treat it as a few months off, a working vacation, and wait for inspiration. I knew I was starting to impress good cricket judges in Zimbabwe, that I must be mature for my age to play for the national side while still at school – but I had absolutely no thought of making a living out of the game. It was still just a game to me then.

Ironically Worcestershire agreed to take me on because I bowled off-spin. They had a small staff at the time and they were short of spinners for their second eleven that summer, so when their secretary Mike Vockins was told by Alwyn Pichanick that I was an off-spinner, he said, 'Good, we could do with him, he'll get a lot of work in the seconds.' He didn't seem all that bothered that I could bat a bit. I've often wondered what would have happened to my career if Alwyn had said I was an opening bat who bowled occasional seamers!

CHAPTER FOUR

A Passage to England

I ARRIVED at Worcester on 2 April 1984 – freezing cold. I couldn't believe that professional cricketers would be out in that sort of weather but sure enough, when I got to New Road, they were in the nets, the first of the new season. The coach, Basil D'Oliveira, suggested I have a bat and, because of the cold, I didn't need to be asked twice. I raced back to the pavilion, teeth chattering, opened up my case of kit – and found I had left all my cricket sweaters back in Zimbabwe! All I had to wear was a white casual jumper made of acrylic, which didn't ward off the cold at all. So I ran back over to the nets, grateful at least for pads and gloves to keep some parts of my body slightly above freezing level.

The first-team players had turned up that day, and they were fairly gentle with me in that first net – putting the ball well up to me for the drive, and not digging it in short. We were on the artificial wicket, so there was no danger of anything whistling around my ears. I was so excited, it was great to stand there, driving the ball straight back at experienced county cricketers. I was slightly in awe of them, because I knew very little about them (apart from Basil D'Oliveira) and assumed they were all very successful. That first net went very well and the next one even better. We were practising out in the middle and Basil was setting us targets, as if we were in a match. He would say, 'Right, four balls to go, twelve to win', and we would go for it. I remember Paul Pridgeon pitched one short at me and I pulled it a long way for six. I was really surprised it went so far. Afterwards, John Inchmore said to me, 'I'm never going to bowl you another half-volley – they keep going straight back over my head!' We still have a laugh about that whenever we meet up.

So the cricket side started off reasonably well, but I was lonely in that first month. I still had it in my mind that England was full of drug addicts and violence, so I didn't venture out of my little world of digs and cricket. I moved into Number 164 Comer Road, near to New Road, and I was very happy there with a lovely couple called Pauline and David Mease. They put me in a little box room at the top of the house and, with just one cupboard and a bed, there was no danger of me throwing my clothes around and making the room untidy! For that first month, I'd stroll to the ground, work hard in the nets and then walk back for an evening huddled round the fire, watching television, polishing off all Pauline's packets of biscuits and drinking coffee. I loved the novelty of TV and just wanted to keep warm. I wrote quite a few letters home after it dawned on me that it would be another six months before I saw my family again. I felt a stranger in a foreign land, and out of my depth away from my digs and the cricket ground, but that was nobody's fault. The Worcestershire players would ask me to go for a drink with them, but I preferred my own company. Boarding school had given me a sense of independence after going through the various trials of strength, and I wasn't going to get too depressed about life in Worcester. I told myself that it would soon pick up once I started playing regular cricket, with (I hoped) some sun on my back.

I was lucky that I managed to play so much cricket that season. It eventually settled down into a long, hot summer (by England's standards!) and I was very happy playing for various sides almost every day. I had come over simply to enjoy the experience, with none of the pressures facing my team-mates, who were looking for a career from the game. I just wanted to score a lot of runs by playing well and then return to Zimbabwe to think about some sort of career. Things went well for me as soon as I got into the county second eleven. I made 49 against Somerset and got out mishitting a spinner straight up in the air. I wasn't too worried about missing out on my fifty, I was just enjoying myself. I saw no reason to play defensively – it made sense to me to play my shots, rather than retreat into my shell. It was a great thrill to stand beside Kapil

Dev at slip in that game, listening to his analysis of batsmen's weaknesses. He told me that one batsman drove 'on the up' and that he would soon be caught at cover, playing uppishly. He was. He forecast that one chap would be either caught and bowled or taken at mid-off: an over later, that happened. I listened a lot to Kapil after that, and I found him excellent value, so positive in his outlook, so intent on enjoying the game. He didn't allow himself to become over-burdened with theories even though he thought a great deal about cricket. He always seemed a very happy person – certainly his game was natural and full of flair – and I think one thing I learned from Kapil was that if you were in the right frame of mind, you had a better chance of going out there and doing well. His example came back to me several times in later years when I wasn't at my best, on and off the field.

In my second game – against Leicestershire – I got a hundred between lunch and tea on the small Old Hill ground. I was soon happy with the cricket, enjoying the travelling to new places, meeting up with my new team-mates, even having the occasional drink in a pub, and letting myself in late at my digs – to grapple with two huge Old English Sheepdogs, who would only stop barking after I'd locked the door behind me. We had some great laughs that summer in the second team. There was the time one night when our scorer, Paul Wintle, was drawn into a drinking session at our hotel with Basil D'Oliveira, a man who is something of a legend in that direction. Basil threw some gin and tonics down Paul's throat and, after half an hour's play the next morning when the first wicket had fallen, we had the sight of our scorer leaning over the steps, emptying his stomach! He then went back to his scoring duties, as we fell about on the field.

I had another enjoyable memory from that game. I scored 170 and during that innings I pulled Bruce Roberts for a couple of sixes. Bruce had been one of my seniors at Prince Edward's a few years earlier, so those two sixes were sweet revenge for all the skivvying duties at school. The most impressive match for me in the second team was the one at New Road against Worcestershire, when Martin Weston and I added almost 400. Martin eventually got a double hundred but I had to make do with 195 and it was my own fault. We were neck and neck in the race to the double hundred, and I kept eyeing the short boundary on the Cathedral side of the ground. John Childs was bowling his left-hand spin at me and I went down on one knee, aiming to lap him for six over the short boundary. Out lbw, and no complaints about the decision. It was silly of me to take the risk and since then I've told myself that when I play the lap shot I must bring the bat down on the ball, rather than aim for hitting the ball over the ropes.

I scored almost a thousand runs for the second team in that 1984 season and, although I averaged over 60, I was happier with the aggregate. I had soon worked my way up from five to three in the batting order and you don't get too many not-outs at number three, to boost the average. To me it was more important to score a lot of runs. I didn't know how well I had done until people at the club started to tell me; I had no idea what constituted a good season at number three for a county second eleven. I didn't set myself any targets, just concentrated on enjoying the adventure. I also bowled more overs than anyone else in the seconds, so I think the club got full value from me! The man who really helped me was the coach, Basil D'Oliveira. He was the only man at New Road I knew much about when I arrived. After flicking through the pages of his autobiography, I was in awe of such a great player. But he never put himself on a pedestal with the younger players – we always thought we could go up to him and talk about anything. He never made us feel uncomfortable about taking up his time. Soon Basil was setting me targets to drive me on. He didn't help me specifically on technique, apart from a few minor suggestions, but he would coax me along by setting me goals. He was very miserly with his praise towards me and I kept wondering why. After I had got a few forties, feeling pretty pleased with myself, he'd say, 'The good players get hundreds, not forties.' Then if I got a hundred, he'd say, 'The good players go on to get big hundreds, they don't get out like you did.' After I got my hundred in one session against Leicestershire seconds, he said, 'Good players can last for more than just a session, you know.' So I'd managed that, and walk past him with a smile on my face, only to be told, 'Good players can bat for two sessions.' Then he'd tell me it was important to bat for a whole day. I felt I just couldn't win with him – when would I get any praise? I now realise that Basil rated me as a batsman, that he only praised those who were operating to the limit of their abilities. On the days when I'd heard him praise someone who had got fifty and ignored my unbeaten hundred, I'd wonder what was going on, but I eventually twigged that he was just motivating me in a different way.

In that first season, just before we played Warwickshire at Edgbaston, Basil wandered past me and said, 'This lot at Warwick don't rate you – they say you never get runs when they watch you.' That was all. I got 143 that day, and I remember hitting Dean Hoffman's slower ball over the pavilion into the road. I was pleased with that and the way I had responded to Basil's goading. It was so important to me to get a good word from him, and that's remained the case. When I scored my 405 not out at Taunton in 1988, I was waiting for him to tell me that good players go on to get five hundred, but he just said, 'Well played.' That meant a lot to me, because he hadn't added a 'but' to his praise.

In recent seasons, he has been very good to me in general advice – how to handle the press, how to prepare myself for Test cricket if I do get picked – and he's very good on the right attitude to the game. In an early match for the seconds, we declared when I got my hundred and I walked off with my partner trailing thirty yards behind me. Yet my partner had also played well to get a half-century and the coach tore a strip off me in the dressing room. He said, 'Don't ever do that again – you must show respect for your partner. It's not a one-man game. He batted harder for his fifty than you did for your hundred and you should acknowledge that.' He was right.

I learned a great deal from Basil that first summer and from just listening to the senior players in the dressing room, if I wasn't playing. I'd go in there to soak up the atmosphere and listen to what the first-team players were saying about the bowling, the wicket and anything else about the game. No one ever threw the coaching book at me when I came to Worcester, but I was lucky that the experienced players were so good at offering insights into what goes on in the middle when jobs are at stake. I was aware that in Zimbabwe the cricket – although hard and competitive – is essentially amateur, so that it's not the end of the world if someone fails for a few weekends on the trot. The English professionals all had to perform, so it was a case for them of grasping every opportunity they could get in the first team. Many of them didn't have a profession to fall back on, and it was interesting to see how different players reacted to that pressure.

Basil D'Oliveira also did me a big favour in my first summer by fixing me up with Kidderminster to play in the Birmingham League. Basil had played for Kidderminster twenty years earlier when qualifying for Worcestershire and he knew the people and the set-up there. He took me there for my first game, introduced me to all the right people and drove me back home at night. Brought up in the vast open spaces of Zimbabwe, I was amazed at how many people live so close to each other in England, with towns on top of one another. When Basil first drove me out to Kidderminster, I thought we were going out to the bush, yet within about ten minutes, we were there. When you consider that it's an hour's drive from the farm to Harare – with just a tiny village in between, and nothing more – you can appreciate that the English summer of 1984 was a learning process in more than just cricket areas. I really enjoyed my season with Kidderminster. After a slow start, I scored over 1200 runs, a record for the club, and they kindly presented me with a silver salver to mark the feat. I was also given a colourful tee-shirt, with the slogan 'Beer Drinkers Have More Guts' and on the back, 'Block – Block – Slog', a reference to my style of batting, according to some of my team-mates. Geoff Parry and Mike Wilkinson used to say I played by numbers, blocking a couple, then hitting a good-length ball for four. I've still got that tee-shirt to remind me of many laughs with the Kidderminster guys. There was a great deal of leg-pulling between us. Geoff Parry has a slightly gammy leg and I used to give him a lot of stick about his running between the wickets. He'd call me 'Slug' (as in slow as a slug), but it was all good fun. The team spirit was excellent – that's always been important to me – and the wicket at

Kidderminster was very good. It still is and, when Worcestershire play an occasional county game there, I'm always amazed that they turn out to be low-scoring matches. It's a pleasure to go back to the club, to thank Godfrey Lamb and Pete Radburn for all the lifts they gave me to strange-sounding places and to remind Pete that I usually hit the ball further than he did, even though he favoured the railway line, while I aimed for the cabbage patch!

By September, I was preparing to return to Zimbabwe after a highly enjoyable time at Worcester. Playing almost every day in a warm summer was no hardship to me, I had scored a lot of runs and on the social front had graduated from that lonely first month to a few regular haunts with my team-mates at Worcester. We had many a laugh and practical joke in wine bars and pubs, and that all helped us enjoy our cricket. Worcestershire was beginning to pull round after several mediocre seasons, and in 1984 several players were pressing for the first team after good performances in the seconds. As for me, I never thought about getting into the first team. The way was blocked by Kapil Dev, but when he returned to India to prepare for a Test series, the way was clear to play another overseas player. So I got a game in our last championship match of the season, at the Oval against Surrey. We also had a few injuries, so they threw me in at the deep end. It was a great experience, and the fact that I scored 82 not out in my only innings made it even more memorable. Before I batted, I pulled a masterstroke. Our captain, Phil Neale, asked for volunteers to do duty in the slips, and I put my hand up right away. I'd managed to sneak in there for Zimbabwe, even though I was young enough to be stationed at bat/pad with all the protective gear on. I enjoyed fielding at slip and when I took a good one to catch Graeme Clinton (above my head at second slip), I had booked my place. I've been there ever since when we are attacking – anyway, I'm too tall for short leg!

When I came in to bat for the first time in championship cricket, we faced defeat. One or two of our players were carrying injuries, and due to the use of a nightwatchman, I ended up at number nine. I also found myself facing Sylvester Clarke, at that time one of the most fearsome fast bowlers around. Sylvester was a nasty prospect, with his steep bounce and the habit of hitting batsmen rather painfully. He was easily the fastest I had faced at that time and as I sat with my pads on, I kept telling myself, 'Stay side-on. If he squares me up, he's got more of a target to hit.' I knew that Sylvester would be looking to clean up the tail when I went in at number nine, so it was a case of getting all the protective gear on and fighting it out.

For a long time I didn't think about playing any attacking shots, and concentrated on getting out of the way. Phil Neale and I simply had to block it out for long periods as we had no chance of setting them a target. After a time, Sylvester went round the wicket – his usual ploy when anyone was blocking him – and Phil and I then had to do a lot of dodging and weaving as the short-pitched stuff kept coming. There was hardly anyone in front of the wicket, apart from those at bat/pad, so if we got a part of the bat on the ball and pierced the field, it usually went to the boundary. Phil Neale had told me that I had to bat for as long as possible and I did that. The game ended half an hour early because of rain and, although many sympathised with me for missing out on a hundred on my championship debut, I wasn't fussed at all. I was more pleased with my performance than with the scores. I had to take myself up a few psychological gears and battle hard against pace I hadn't experienced. It was a very interesting day for me. I told myself not to freeze, to play the man not his reputation – even though Sylvester himself was pretty fearsome on the day! I was very happy with my first fifty runs, because they had had to be chiselled out, but after that the tension eased a little as Surrey brought on their occasional bowlers near the end.

Until that game at the Oval, I hadn't been really aware of the international class of men like Clarke, Geoff Howarth or Pat Pocock – they were just names to me. The gulf in class compared to the second eleven was very noticeable. In the seconds, you're usually playing with and against young men, whereas in the first team you're with mature men who play cricket for a profession and therefore take it seriously. Even though I had played with adults in Zimbabwe for a few years, the Oval game made me realise what was involved in championship cricket. Although many had praised me for my performances with the second team and for Kidderminster, I hadn't got carried away, because the standard of club cricket in Zimbabwe was just as good. The local Worcester paper had noted a few of my big scores and I had dutifully cut them out and mailed them off to my parents for their scrapbook, but I was just happy to have done myself justice, while treating the whole thing as fun. That game at the Oval marked an important part of my development.

A week before my championship debut, the club had asked me to come back for another season. I was keen. The club's supporters and officials had made me more aware of my potential; the kind words in the local newspaper made for pleasant reading and I assumed the writers knew enough about the game to hand out praise when they felt it was justifiable. They couldn't all be wrong, could they? Even Basil D'Oliveira had offered an occasional 'Well played' towards the end of the season, so I must have had something to offer. When Worcestershire offered me a contract for 1985, I was really pleased. I was beginning to think that a career in county cricket might be a very pleasant prospect, not least because I had little going for me in other careers. I was conscious that my parents had encouraged me just to enjoy the 1984 season, and then think about what I was going to do with the rest of my life.

I had done just that, but I had also managed to gain my NCA coaching certificate at the National Sports Centre at Lilleshall. At the time I applied for the course, I wasn't thinking about coming back to Worcester – it had seemed a good idea to get some sort of qualification that might impress the cricket authorities in Zimbabwe. I found the cricket aspect of the course easy enough, but it was hard whenever I was pulled out to demonstrate certain techniques to the rest of the class. They mainly consisted of adult teachers, used to talking confidently to a classroom of children, while I was a shy eighteen-year-old who knew what I wanted to say, but didn't express myself terribly well. Running the coaching session for ten minutes was a good deal harder for me than batting for hours in the nets, but I managed to get my certificate. If all else failed, I could at least offer my coaching qualification to anyone who might be looking for someone who wanted to work in cricket.

So I rang my parents and discussed Worcestershire's offer. As we always do whenever an important decision in my life is called for, we discussed the pros and cons for a long time and they went away to work out their attitude. It's been a great consolation to know that my parents don't give me advice they think I'd like to hear – they make up their own minds and talk honestly to me. This time, they thought I should accept the offer from Worcestershire and try to see how far I could go in the English professional game. I would be nineteen at the end of the 1985 season and that was hardly in the veteran class when it came to looking for another career if this failed. After that innings against Surrey, I was even more excited at the prospect of another season at New Road. Another hurdle had presented itself at just the right moment and I had got over it. I felt I had the ability to do well, it was just a case of getting myself mentally right to keep delivering the goods. Now I wasn't afraid of first-class cricket after my baptism of fire at the hands of Sylvester Clarke; I would go quietly about the business of learning my trade, and try to surmount every important challenge that came along. With a man like Basil D'Oliveira at my side, there would be no danger of my getting big ideas about myself. I felt that if he thought I could go places in the professional game, then I owed it to myself to give it a go.

I went back to Zimbabwe, full of optimism that I could get a good season under my belt to prepare myself for the Worcestershire experience, but I didn't do myself justice over the next few months. For some reason I kept getting out when well set, and I couldn't turn a good start into a major innings. Early in the Zimbabwean season, we played several games against the touring New Zealanders, a strong side containing the likes of Jeff Crowe, Martin Snedden, Ken Rutherford, John Bracewell and Bruce Edgar. I was now firmly installed at number three in the senior Zimbabwe team, but I wasn't all that prolific. John Bracewell trapped me lbw for 95 in one game, as I tried to force the pace, knowing that Andy Pycroft wouldn't be coming out to keep an end up, as he felt ill. My dismissal was bad judgement on my part – hitting across the line – but it would have been unfair to expect my partner, Kevin Duers, to hang around for too long. Pycroft, a good enough batsman, could have done that easily, but he wasn't well enough.

A week later, I was out for 88 against the Kiwis, playing defensively to a ball that left me, to give a catch to the wicket-keeper. I was got out, rather than getting myself out, and I was still short of my maiden hundred for Zimbabwe. It was just as frustrating against an English Counties side that came over a few months later. I kept getting myself out for reasonable scores, but not enough for the standards I was starting to set myself. It was a matter of concentration, something you can only pick up as you go along. It's not something you can teach, like the off-drive, you have to experience it.

The English Counties side under Mark Nicholas were a good test, because they bowled straight and really made us work hard for our runs. After my experience in second-eleven cricket (where you could count on at least one bad ball per over), I was looking for loose deliveries from bowlers like Nick Cook, Neil Williams and Tim Tremlett that just weren't there. We were more impressive in the limited-overs games against the tourists, because we fielded brilliantly and bowled pretty straight, but the longer tempo of the three-day matches seemed to suit the English players more. We played mainly sixty overs a side at the time and the longer form of cricket found us lacking in the necessary concentration – myself included. I'm glad to say that no one had made a big fuss of me when I returned to Zimbabwe after my first good season at Worcester. Of course I had developed as a cricketer in England, but I was still no more than promising. It was, after all, second-eleven cricket I had played and just one innings for the first team was hardly something to get excited about in Harare. I was treated the same way as before in the bar of the Harare Sports Club, and I wouldn't have had it any other way.

By the end of that season, another challenge had presented itself. Our national side was to tour England, to get more experience for the following year's ICC Trophy. I was picked for the tour, which meant I would be dividing the English season up between playing for Zimbabwe and for Worcestershire. Again, a fresh hurdle had appeared and at the age of nineteen I was eager to jump over it.

CHAPTER FIVE

The Learning Curve

THE 1985 summer in England did a lot to persuade me to believe I might have some sort of future in professional cricket. From the early weeks when I scored a few hundreds for the second team at New Road, things went my way. When the Zimbabwean tour party joined me in June, I made some big scores, then towards the end of the season I broke into the Worcestershire first team and scored a couple of championship hundreds. In first-class cricket alone, I scored over a thousand runs, and I was also pleased by the fact that the lowest of my four hundreds was 128. Even at the age of nineteen, I saw no point in giving it away once I'd reached three figures. By September, I was a good deal clearer in my mind about my long-term ambitions and what I had to do to achieve them.

That Zimbabwe tour lasted almost two months and it was another hugely enjoyable trip, despite the rainy weather. Again we played good cricket even though lacking six of the 1983 World Cup squad. Peter Rawson, our fine swing bowler, had changed jobs and couldn't get time off for the trip, our all-rounder Kevin Curran had opted for county cricket with Gloucestershire and two of our best batters, Duncan Fletcher and Jack Heron, had emigrated. Andy Pycroft also had to return home early for the birth of his first child. But we still acquitted ourselves well, and the party picked up vital experience for the following year's ICC Trophy. The long-term aim in 1985 was selection of Zimbabwe for the World Cup, to be held in Pakistan and India towards the end of 1987. To qualify, we had to win the 1986 ICC Trophy in England. Zimbabwe managed that, but the 1985 tour was crucial to the preparation. All the one-day games were won and that kind of matchplay experience in different conditions is invaluable.

I was in very good nick when I met up with the team. I had just scored 187 against Glamorgan seconds, so when we started our tour at Oxford, I was seeing the ball very early. On a soft, slow wicket against a fairly friendly University attack, I made 230. During the match it was confirmed that the game would have first-class status, so I was delighted to record my maiden hundred and then make it a double. I had been told that batting at Oxford was a dream once you had your eye in, and, although the University bowling wasn't very taxing, I was pleased with my concentration. I batted almost five hours for those runs – easily the longest period I'd yet spent at the crease – and I just concentrated on putting away the bad balls. There were a few of them! By then, it was starting to dawn on me that one of the hardest aspects of batting is the mental test, staying in for long periods, making yourself concentrate even harder as your innings goes into another hour. It is fair to say that I had faced bigger batting tests in my short career than the one at Oxford, but I kept going and that was important.

The same applied in our next first-class game, against Glamorgan, when I scored 192. Again I batted for over four hours, and even though Glamorgan didn't play many of their first-team men, I still had to get them against county bowlers, rather than university students. I came in very early, and settled down to enjoy myself on a flat wicket. The batting part of it wasn't all that hard – it was more taxing to steel myself to compile a big innings, with time not a factor, as it was in most of my cricket in Zimbabwe at the time. I wanted another double hundred and I was annoyed at myself for getting out – cutting loosely at the slow left-arm spinner, to be caught in the gully. I caught it on the top edge and the fielder had to dive forward to catch it. I thought to myself, 'He isn't going to catch that,' but he did and I had to drag myself away.

I was reminded of the importance of building an innings in the next match, at Edgbaston when we played Warwickshire. In that game, Dennis Amiss reached 40,000 runs in first-class cricket, and he kindly provided champagne to celebrate with both teams. Even with my scant knowledge of cricket history, I knew that 40,000 runs at the top level was an enormous amount, a tribute to the man's hunger and love of the game, apart from his obvious natural batting talent. As I stood there, sipping champagne from a man I had only admired from a distance, I wondered what was involved in such an achievement. I had not even reached a thousand runs in first-class cricket at that stage, and I just couldn't believe the dedication involved from Dennis. Now that I am more established in the first-class game, I can see it as something I'd be really proud to achieve. Such consistency says a lot about what you have put into your profession.

A fortnight later, I came up against the kind of fast bowling barrage that Dennis Amiss had had to face a few years earlier from the likes of Lillee, Thomson, Holding and Roberts. We played the League Cricket Conference at Middleton, up in Lancashire, and the batsmen were really put through the mincer by Tony Merrick and Winston Benjamin. Both West Indian fast bowlers have since made quite a name for themselves in county cricket, but at that time they were raw, eager to make an impression – and very quick. We started our innings in the last hour of the first day, and Ali Shah and Grant Paterson soon had to dodge and weave as it got darker. One ball from Merrick went right across the face of Ali Shah before he had even moved. Luckily, Ali was a left-hander and it whizzed past his nose, but if he had been a right-hander Merrick's natural in-slant would have pinned him right between the eyes. Merrick was roaring in down the slope and really letting it go, and when Grant asked Ali what it was like at his end, he received the classic comment, 'It's brisk man, bloody brisk!' That remark kept us chuckling for weeks.

When I came in to bat, I just concentrated on occupying the crease. Merrick bowled slightly off the wrong foot, so the ball speared in at the right-hander to take you by surprise. He didn't exactly believe in pitching the ball up – he was too keen on seeing us hop about – so there was no chance of me unfurling a flowing drive or two. With the hook shot never on my batting menu (too risky, the ball's in the air too long for my liking), I just had to duck or play at the ball if it was jagging in at me. As soon as Merrick banged it in, I knew I didn't need to play a shot because it was never going to hit the stumps. But such decisions had to be made pretty swiftly against two very awkward bowlers, and it took some time to adjust to the speed. It proved to be a very useful initiation for me though, because I knew that every county side had a fast bowler like Merrick, possibly two of them operating in tandem. At some stage I would have to get used to all that if I was to have any prospect of getting runs in the county championship. Double hundreds at Oxford, although very desirable, don't help you much when the light is bad and a hulking West Indian is roaring in at you.

That trip was educational in more senses than just cricket. We saw a fair amount of Britain, playing in Wales and Scotland as well – so the camera had an outing or two. We younger members of the tour party also discovered the joys of drinking Scotch and ginger ale. On our days off, I enjoyed my evenings with Eddo Brandes (an old schoolmate), Ali Shah and Ian Butchard, and I somehow forgot all my obsessions about crime and drugs in Britain, so that a trip to the bar came to seem a very sensible idea. Nothing excessive – I still don't drink all that much – but a nice way to broaden the palate, trying out various ways to take Scotch. Before our game at Arundel towards the end of the tour, our manager, David Ellman-Brown, said at the team meeting, 'Never in my life have I seen so much Scotch drunk by so many young people.' Rather harsh, we thought, but it definitely constituted a slap on the wrists. All the younger members of the squad looked sheepishly at one another while the older ones tried not to laugh. We had a great team spirit on that tour, even though a few of us were a fair bit younger than the rest. But we all mixed in at the right moments, one of the most important requirements of any cricket side.

Within a couple of weeks of the end of that Zimbabwe tour, I was playing championship cricket for Worcestershire. The fact that Kapil Dev had to return early to India for Test duty did me no harm and a place in the middle order opened up for me. Although I enjoyed batting at three for Zimbabwe I had no right to expect anything higher than number six for Worcestershire, with Phil

Neale, Dipak Patel and David Smith all good, experienced players and deserving to bat ahead of me. Eventually I got in at number three in September and that's where I scored my two championship hundreds. The first, against Somerset, was really exciting. I got 174 not out, sharing in two big stands with Tim Curtis and Phil Neale for the first time. I love batting with both players, and in recent years we have shared many big stands. Both are cool professionals with excellent cricket brains. They're very good at working out the run-rate (they have both been schoolteachers, so they should be!) and at spotting weaknesses in the bowlers. Tim and Phil are good encouragers, very supportive partners and we complement each other well. They do the thinking, I do the batting!

In that Somerset game, I came up against Joel Garner for the first time and all my feelings of foreboding I had about him in the World Cup of 1983 were borne out. At the start of his run-up, he looked about six feet from that distance, but when he got to the crease, he looked enormous. I seemed to do nothing but play the ball in front of my nose or get whacked on the inside of the left thigh. I was sore in that area that evening, but delighted with my innings. It was a big one, too; I saw no point in getting out just after I got my hundred, when there was still plenty of time available to my team at the crease. I knew even then that there would be plenty of times when I'd get cleaned up for nought, so why not cash in on the hard work when you can?

After that innings, a lot of people came up to me and said they were surprised I had got a championship hundred so quickly, that it normally takes a long time to adjust to the demands of the top-class game. But I felt I had the ability in me, and I was really excited at doing something I'd wanted to achieve ever since playing at the Oval the season before. I was delighted that I'd managed to keep out the demon Garner yorker (I don't get yorked all that often, despite the high backlift), and it meant a great deal to me that I had outscored Phil and Tim, two players I had learned to respect greatly already in my time at New Road.

My second championship hundred was made in circumstances that weren't quite so testing as facing Joel Garner. David Capel and Roger Harper were the only two front-line bowlers in the Northants attack, but I was still happy at reaching the landmark. It was all so new to me, I was playing for sheer enjoyment. I just went out and batted and each game brought a fresh challenge because all the bowlers were new to me. It was great to know that I could go up a notch against proper county attacks. I seemed to be getting better at the English professional game, learning how to play differently on various wickets, how to cope with specific bowlers, how to handle a run chase. I had no particular targets in mind – apart from trying to get to three figures if I was anywhere near – and it was a thrill to be on the same field as so many great players.

It was a fantastic experience to bowl at Viv Richards during his hundred against us at Taunton. I even had a stumping chance missed off my bowling! When the captain brought me on, I ventured the opinion that Viv was playing so well that it didn't really matter where I bowled at him, because it would probably disappear. So I decided to give it a bit of air, in the hope that the ball would turn. It did, and Viv was stranded as the ball turned square, but Steve Rhodes couldn't quite manage what would have been a great stumping. I wasn't a good enough bowler to trouble Viv, but what a player! Some say he's not a textbook batsman, but from what I have seen at close quarters everything is in the right place when he hits the ball. When he whips the ball through midwicket, he still plays it with a straight bat and a still head, and doesn't fall over. He stands upright at the crease, his wrists are amazingly strong and his eyesight must be phenomenal. When I caught him at slip in the first innings, I felt pretty elated at dismissing such a great player.

I don't suppose Derek Underwood batted an eyelid when he clean bowled me in the Kent match that season, but I shan't forget the ball in a hurry. I played the perfect forward defensive stroke to him, except that the ball pitched on middle and leg and hit the off-stump! I didn't get a bat on it and that ball made me understand what it must have been like to try to keep out Underwood in his heyday on a wet wicket. But my biggest memory of that short championship season must be facing Joel Garner. In that innings, he still sent down the occasional quicker ball, which really got me on the move. I found myself wondering what it would be like batting day after day against those who bowl consistently as fast as Garner did at times that day.

That was the next stage to go through but, for now, I was really happy with my second season at New Road. It was an exciting time for me, with so many fresh experiences crowding in on me, and it was also a great time for the younger Worcestershire players, as a good side started to emerge. Players like Phil Newport, Tim Curtis, Steve Rhodes, Martin Weston, Richard Illingworth and Damian D'Oliveira were all growing up together and when we won our first championship in 1988 it was lovely to feel part of a revival that had begun a few years earlier. In 1985, we all seemed to be learning the game at the same time. Almost every day, someone was buying us drinks in the bar for getting a career best with either the bat or the ball. As for me, I wasn't yet at the stage where I had to tell myself I just had to get runs that day, to cut out various shots that might be risky; I just went out there and batted instinctively, with hardly a worry. The new boy is never expected to be the matchwinner, so whatever he achieves is a bonus. No pressure, just a lot of fun. And the start of some great friendships, especially with Damian D'Oliveira, who has been my room-mate on away trips ever since that 1985 season. We share the same sense of humour, love of golf, fondness for sleep and reluctance to get out of bed in the morning. For a time, Dolly's fondness for cigarettes caused me bronchial trouble in an enclosed hotel room, so he cut down on his nicotine intake. Now he smokes small cigars, which suits his status as a devoted family man!

So if the 1984 English season whetted my appetite, 1985 opened it all up for me. I took stock of myself at the end of the 1985 season and realised that the terrific experience of the last month had made me hungry for the professional game. I now wanted to kick on, to see just what I could do. Batting against Test bowlers hadn't found me out, and I had relished the challenge of going up a few gears against them. I had looked around at the top players in the county championship and tried to see what I could learn from them. Obviously mental discipline, the need to occupy the crease for long periods. The concentration involved in waiting for the bad ball, and then putting it away; as I have said, at this level the bad balls are not frequent. It all seemed to come down to one thing – physical fitness. I realised that if you are very fit, you can hold your concentration at the crease that much longer.

So when I returned to Zimbabwe, I went into a gym, vowing to get fit for my chosen profession. Worcestershire wanted me back next season – Kapil Dev would be touring England with India – and I was determined to make an early, positive impression in my first full season of county cricket. The gym was run by Ian Robertson, who used to play rugby for the Springboks, and he put me through a punishing routine that involved weights to get me stronger and running to build up my stamina. In the gym there were a few signs on the wall and I had to agree with their message: 'Success Comes to Those Who Are Success-Conscious' and 'If You're Physically Fit, You're Mentally Fit'. It was clear to me that you'll get out what you put in, whatever career you choose – and now I wanted to get a lot out of English cricket. The old vagueness of a future career had gone and I could point to two years of solid advance to my parents as proof that I really felt I could now make a living from cricket. They trusted my judgement.

Over the next few months, my batting became more consistent as I got fitter and stronger. I got my maiden first-class hundred in Zimbabwe, against a Young Australia side, containing Dean Jones, Bruce Reid, Steve Waugh, Mike Veletta, Dave Gilbert and Tony Dodemaide. Early in 1986, I scored 309 against the touring Ireland team, and there's a story or two about that innings. The tour had been organised by my father, and the Irish were very sociable cricketers who fitted in perfectly with the hospitable Zimbabwean way of life. They did have one small complaint, though; they felt the opposition wasn't strong enough, too many games were finishing early, which meant even more time in the bar. Dad was a little embarrassed at this, so he asked me to turn out in a couple of games against the Irish. I scored 155 not out against them in a one-day game, then the following day, playing for the President's Eleven, I ended up with another unbeaten hundred. We batted on the next day (it was a three-day match) and I was finally caught at long-off by a chap called John Prior. John had dropped me at short midwicket when I had only scored fourteen – it was an easy chance and he got more and more depressed as I carried on enjoying myself. When he finally caught me for 309, he was absolutely thrilled, throwing the ball up in the air, yelping with delight and going on a lap of honour! Everyone took it in good part – they were great guys to play against – and they begged Dad not to pick me against them again. Incidentally Dad reckons that 309 was the fiftieth hundred I had scored in all forms of cricket. At the time, I could barely remember twenty of them.

By the spring of 1986, life couldn't have been happier for me. After working hard in the gym, I was reaping the benefits of extra stamina and improved concentration. I couldn't wait to measure my progress over an entire season of county cricket, where many world-class cricketers would be lining up against me. With the greatest respect to the Irish bowlers and the Oxford students, I knew that scores of 309 and 230 were impressive on paper, but didn't add up to much if you were trying to assess my real worth as a batsman. That would come week in, week out in the hard, professional English world. Another hurdle was there for me to try to clear – but first I had to make a tricky decision about my future. I knew it was the most important one so far of my cricket career, and I had to get it right.

CHAPTER SIX

Why I Chose England

IN April 1986 I made the most important decision of my career. I decided to qualify for England in the hope of playing Test cricket some day. Some might say that I was turning my back on Zimbabwe after great support from the Cricket Union, but, after serious consideration, the pros on England's side far outweighed those in favour of Zimbabwe. Before the end of the 1985 English season, I had been discussing the possibility of qualifying for England with Worcestershire's chairman, Duncan Fearnley, and the secretary, Mike Vockins. They believed that I was good enough eventually to play for England, they were also conscious that if I qualified, the club would stand to gain from my loss of status as an overseas player. As administrators, they would obviously look to the future, and they felt that if I lost my overseas classification, they could then go into the market for a big name and strengthen the Worcestershire squad. I could see the sense in that, although my own decision was based entirely on my desire to play Test cricket for England. Yet at the back of my mind was the thought that if I managed to qualify for England, I wouldn't be keeping out an overseas player, as had happened when Kapil Dev and I were competing for one place in my early days at New Road.

I knew there were precedents for clubs chopping off their current overseas player; counties tend to move for a fast bowler if he becomes available and a batsman might be deemed surplus to requirements. So if I qualified for England, that would at least prolong my county career, even if I never made the grade at Test level. So my decision made sense for Worcestershire, but for me it was largely a case of professional ambition. In my first two seasons at New Road, I had played at Test match grounds like Lord's, the Oval and Old Trafford and I had noticed there was a buzz about such places. I was very lucky to be playing county cricket at one of the nicest grounds in the country, but I also wondered what it must be like to walk out and bat in front of a packed Test ground. I had no idea if I would be good enough to play for England, but I felt I owed it to myself to take steps towards realising that dream. I didn't want to be kicking myself in years to come, wondering what would have happened if I had broken with Zimbabwe's national side. There was a clear, simple choice for me: I had to aim for England qualification and forget about ever playing again for Zimbabwe. That meant pulling out of the tour party due to leave for England to take part in the ICC Trophy.

At that time, I was well aware that I would face a wait of up to ten years before becoming eligible for England. I was prepared for that, even though Mike Vockins did try to establish a link with England via my parents. My dad sent Mike a copy of *Debrett's Illustrated Baronetage* to see if there was any connection with England. The nearest he got was that my great-grandfather (Charles Henry Vincent Baskerville) was born at sea and eventually lived in Liverpool, and that my mum's grandfather (Charles Hubert Noble) was born in Yorkshire. That wasn't enough to establish a direct qualification for England, so I had to settle for ten years' consecutive residence in England for a substantial part of each year – later set at 210 days a year. So we established that I would be first available for England in 1994 – ten years on from April 1984 when I first arrived at Worcester. I had no qualms about that. I accepted that there had to be strict rules, otherwise everyone born abroad who fancied playing for England could just walk straight into contention with hardly the bat of an eyelid. Later my qualification period was reduced to seven years (that applied to everyone else with similar ambitions), but I would still have served out the ten years if I had to. The fact that I was ready to turn my back on playing in the 1987 World Cup for Zimbabwe against all the Test countries must surely indicate that I was perfectly aware of the complexities of the situation.

The only opposition I encountered in Zimbabwe to my decision came from two very influential administrators of the Zimbabwe Cricket Union. When I told the president Alwyn Pichanick of my plans, he told me that he would have to try to change my mind. He would offer me a financial package to stay with Zimbabwean cricket, something unheard of in that country. A lot of money was involved but I told him I wasn't interested in the financial aspects – it was a challenge I just had to face. What I wanted I couldn't get in Zimbabwe. He said he understood that, and proceeded to offer me more money! I had always respected Alwyn for what he had done for me and for the country's cricket, and after failing to budge me in his presidential capacity, he said, 'Speaking as a friend, and it's very hard for me to say this, if you want to play Test cricket, then you're making the right move.' We shook hands, and shortly afterwards, I went back to Worcester to prepare for the 1986 season.

Soon after I got there, I had a phone call from Harare and had to deal with a double act trying to talk me out of it – Alwyn Pichanick had been joined by the ZCU Vice-President, Dave Ellman-Brown. Dave had been my manager on several Zimbabwe tours and we had seemed to get on very well, but now I observed a different side to him. Over the phone, he really tore into me and after he had waffled away for a time, I interrupted him with a question: 'Dave, if I was your son, would you stop me trying to play Test cricket?' He said that he would! I said, 'Do you mean that you'd be happy about your son sitting at home for the rest of his life, wondering what might have been? That's absolute rubbish. He'd always hold it against you.' I told him how much I appreciated what the ZCU had done for me, but that there was a time when you have to move on in life, if you have ambitions. What professional cricketer doesn't want to play Test cricket, whatever his ability? Dave wouldn't buy that one at all and, in the end, I realised that our conversation was getting us nowhere and so asked to be put back to Alwyn. So the phone call didn't end very pleasantly, and they were obviously upset that they hadn't talked me out of a decision that had been reached after a lot of thought and consultation with my parents.

Dave told my family how disappointed he was, and that was

understandable enough, but then asked them to repay the amount paid out by the ZCU for the cricket scholarship to go to England. This was duly done and so at the end of the day it was my parents who assisted me in furthering my cricket career. So feelings were unfortunately strained at home between Dave and my family but eventually common sense prevailed when it was realised that I had made the correct decision and things returned to normality, though I must admit I was annoyed that Mum and Dad should have borne the brunt of the affair while I was away in Worcester.

I did have the backing of many cricket supporters in Harare as they stopped my parents in the street expressing their full support for my decision and one person actually went as far as to say that he was considering withdrawing his financial support from national cricket if it went any further. Fortunately this did not take place as the home Union needs all the support they can attract to enable them to continue the good work they are doing to further cricket in Zimbabwe.

My name was also mud in the columns of the *Harare Herald* after the news was broken. I had been short-listed for the Zimbabwe Sportsman of the Year Award, but then the paper stated that I shouldn't be considered for it, now that I had decided not to play any more for Zimbabwe. After meetings among cricket officials, my name was withdrawn from the voting list. I was upset and disappointed. That award would have meant a great deal to me because I still felt a Zimbabwean, even though I was in the process of altering my citizenship. I tried to be philosophical about it, telling myself that the *Herald* had never seemed too supportive towards my club, Old Hararians, and that such incidents were the price to be paid for setting out to qualify for England. I am glad to say that apart from Dave Ellman-Brown's hostility and continued indifference from the *Harare Herald* in my subsequent career, I have had no hassles from anyone back in Zimbabwe. The general reaction has been along the lines of 'Good luck to you, we'll follow your progress.' Many have promised that they'll be in the crowd when – and if – I make my England debut, and that means a lot to me. In fact the overwhelming positive response from the Zimbabwe public towards me gave me an even bigger incentive to do well for Worcestershire. No one has to tell me how much I owe to the officials of Zimbabwean cricket for my development as a player, but I resented the pressure that was placed on my parents once I had made a career decision after long consideration.

I have been asked many times what I would have done if Test status for Zimbabwe had been a possibility in 1986, when I had to make my decision. The answer is I might have been tempted to stay with Zimbabwe. We would still have had a reasonable side, and the good showing in the 1987 World Cup demonstrated that there were some good players still available. Some of those who had gone to play Currie Cup cricket in South Africa would have been tempted back, and although the Zimbabwean Government might have been difficult to deal with over such qualification, something like a two-year residential condition wouldn't have been a great hardship if Test cricket lay at the end of it. That would have been a little more rigorous demand than consuming a crate of Castle Lager and four rump steaks over a weekend in Harare, but still a reasonable attraction to those now living in South Africa. Yet even in 1986 I wanted to pit myself in the long term against the world's best, and in some quantity. I had enjoyed so much batting against those great bowlers in English county cricket that I was curious to see how I would do at the highest level and I was prepared to sit it out to discover if I was up to it.

I was aware that if Zimbabwe had managed to secure Test status, they would have been treated in the same way as Sri Lanka for a long time. A schedule of one Test and a couple of one-day internationals per tour would have been the limit, as Sri Lanka found out throughout much of the 1980s. Then, if you are lucky, the new Test country graduates to a three-Test series. In my two seasons in England, I had seen how the whole summer is geared around the Test series of five or six matches and several one-day internationals as well. That's what I wanted, to be part of that supreme challenge, which lasts over most of the summer, rather than just getting a hint of it, as Sri Lanka have done over the past decade. I noticed that great players like Richard Hadlee and Martin Crowe have never played in a five-Test series, and look how well New Zealand have done for the past few years. Surely they deserved a full summer in England? Yet in 1986 they had to share six Tests with India, while the Australians and the West Indies had an entire series to themselves in England once every four years. Zimbabwe could never expect to break into that sort of status in the course of my career, never mind in the 1980s. After all, both India and New Zealand have been coming to England for more than sixty years, and they still haven't broken into the elite, in the eyes of those who allocate Test series.

I had no doubts that England offered me the best chance of seeing how far I could go in cricket. At the end of my career, I want to say that I have given myself the best chance of succeeding in the professional game – that means, hopefully, being tested out by the West Indies fast bowlers, playing in front of those hostile crowds in Australia, coping with the turning pitches of India and Pakistan. If you're going to be judged as a top batsman, you have to score hundreds in those circumstances, and if I do fail, well at least I can say I tried. I'm the kind of person who wants to do something well if I try it, whether it's golf, cricket, driving a car or whatever. When I leave cricket, I want to walk away from it having made something of a mark for myself if possible. I don't want to leave the game unfulfilled and I sympathise with all those great South African cricketers who lost the chance of development because of political matters beyond their control. I look at batsmen like Graeme Pollock and Barry Richards and all-rounders like Mike Procter and Clive Rice and wonder what they must feel about those wasted years. I didn't want that kind of frustration. I had no idea if I would be good enough for Test cricket eventually, although I was gratified by kind words from people I considered to be good judges of a young player. For me, the cardinal sin would be not trying for it.

I haven't been frustrated in my years of qualification. I knew the score and was delighted when the ten-year period was reduced to seven years by the Test and County Cricket Board in 1989. That was a bonus, because I had been geared to 1994, now it was down to 1991. Mike Vockins has been brilliant with the administrative aspects, telling me to sign one or two things at various times, and just getting me to concentrate on my cricket while he looks after the small print. If ever a minor matter crops up and I ask him about it, he'll say, 'Oh, I dealt with that a month ago.' Mike knows that paper work isn't one of my strong points! Once the decision was made and the necessary documents signed, I simply settled down to learn as much as I could about the game's pressures while I qualified for England. There'd be enough time for worries about the goldfish bowl of Test cricket once I became eligible – for the moment, in 1986, I needed to show I might have something to offer the England selectors in the 1990s. My first full season with Worcestershire was to be an important, historic landmark for me.

CHAPTER SEVEN

Breaking Records

I STARTED the 1986 season unsure if I would be an automatic selection in the Worcestershire side and ended it in a blaze of scoring that established a new record. I became the youngest player to score 2000 first-class runs in a season, beating the record set by Len Hutton almost fifty years earlier. More and more people came up to me and said, 'You know, I saw Hutton bat,' but although I respected his record and stature, it didn't mean all that much to me: I was just doing my job. I'm sure that when my career is over, the achievements of 1986 will have a bigger impact on me.

At the start of the season, it had been made clear to me that I shouldn't expect to play every first-team match. Our other overseas player, Ricky Elcock, had shown great promise as a fast bowler and the thinking was that he would play if the pitch looked like favouring him and I would get in if it was a flat one. That all seemed pretty logical to me and I wasn't too fussed. In our first championship match, I scored a hundred against Surrey and our next game was against the Indian tourists. With David Smith withdrawing on the morning of the Indian game with an injured ankle, they played me as well as Ricky to strengthen the batting (you could play both overseas men against the tourists). I wanted to do well against the Indians because the media were beginning to take notice of me after I had decided to qualify for England and I was looking to make a positive impression. On a wicket that helped the seamers, I felt I played really well to get 70. I hit the rare loose deliveries, left a lot outside the off-stump and played tightly.

That innings pleased me and must have impressed the team

selectors at New Road, because I stayed in the side ahead of Ricky after that. He got the nod over me just once that season, against Sussex in June, and it wasn't handled very well. I could still see why Ricky would be preferred to me in certain circumstances, but looking at the wicket for the Sussex game, I couldn't believe it would be this time. Just one glance at it made me believe it was going to be a flat one, ideal for batsmen and so it turned out – Ricky took one wicket in the game. On the first morning I could tell from the attitude of the team selectors that I would be dropped because no one was looking me in the eye or talking very much to me. Due to a communications breakdown between Basil D'Oliveira and Phil Neale, I wasn't told about being dropped until late on and it was rather embarrassing for them. I remember walking around the ground and being asked why I wasn't playing; all I could say was 'I've been dropped, it's nothing to do with me.' It was the lack of logic behind the decision that stood out. Ricky and I never had a cross word in our time together at New Road and I was sorry when he chose to go to Middlesex after qualifying for England – but trying to establish myself in the first team ahead of him didn't do me any harm.

In that first full championship season, I batted at number four, behind Tim Curtis, Damian D'Oliveira and David Smith. I was perfectly happy with that, coming in behind an experienced player like David Smith with the ball that little bit older. Gaining experience was the main objective for me – I didn't set any targets. I would happily have settled for 2000 first-class runs when I began that season but I was only going for that in the last game when I needed just over a hundred to get there. Before then, it was more important to find out what it was like to bat against the likes of Malcolm Marshall, Michael Holding and Richard Hadlee.

As luck would have it, I batted against those three in successive games and it was an education. Marshall got me out twice in my first encounter with him, the second time for nought. It wasn't a bad way to notch my first championship duck – I went back, played far too late as the ball cut back and it hit the top of the off-stump. The stump cartwheeled a long way back and I thought, 'That's good enough for me.' I was just done for pace. It was all Duncan Fearnley's fault. The night before, our chairman was gloating in the bar at Marshall, because we had just bowled them out cheaply. 'We've done you again,' said Duncan, while our batsmen – including me – thought, 'Shut up, Duncan, you'll get Malcolm fired up.' All he did was smile and say, 'It's not over yet,' and because of him, we lost four wickets getting just over a hundred to win. For some reason, our supporters used to get Malcolm's dander up as well, so he bowled all morning to take the four wickets. He bowled quickly, with variety and control and it was also noticeable that he made us all play at nearly everything. In both innings, I just planned to stay in and see him off, trying to get down to the other end, looking to deflect runs off him rather than even think about going for the hook. He was just too fast and clever for that. Even now, I would remain wary of Malcolm Marshall, although he has lost some of his pace. If you start taking him for granted, he'll slip in something as quick as you've ever received from him. Not as consistently fast as he once was, but still a great bowler.

At that stage in my development, my initial instinct was to go slightly forward, while making sure it didn't become a lunge. In the next match, at Derby, I altered that because the wicket was so unreliable. In the first over, Michael Holding bowled one that reared up off a length and hit Tim Curtis under the chin. Next over, Damian D'Oliveira was bowled by Alan Warner, so I walked in with us 0 for 1 and Tim laid out. I decided to go back and across to Holding, and ended up playing just a handful of shots off the front foot in my innings. I was really pleased to battle my way to 94, but credit must go to Holding for his sportsmanship. After hitting Tim Curtis, he noticeably slowed down and pitched the ball further up. At full throttle on that pitch, he would have been lethal. He was still a handful, though – although bowling a good line and length, the ball would still come through at shoulder height, moving away off the seam. I played and missed at a lot of deliveries that left me, but I didn't let it bother me. It was very satisfying to battle through against a bowler of Holding's class.

In the next game, Richard Hadlee got me out for nought,

caught behind as soon as I came in. I got a faint edge playing off the back foot and spent the next day wondering if Hadlee would do me again: would I get a pair? Luckily, that's something that has so far eluded me and I soon got off the mark in the second innings. I did rather better – my first championship double hundred, 227 not out to be precise. Hadlee didn't bowl many overs in the second innings, but it was still fascinating to bat against him. Like the other great fast bowlers, he rarely varied from nagging line and length and, every now and then, a surprise fast one would let you know his capabilities. In that innings, I pulled one from him to the midwicket boundary, but the next short one was two yards faster, and the ball was through me before I could finish the pull shot.

Although basically a bowler who moved it off the seam, Hadlee could also swing it and he was always at you. He used to do Damian D'Oliveira for a pastime with the ball that nipped back off the seam and I could see why he could dismiss the best players. That double hundred gave me a lot of pleasure – not just because I was on a pair, or that Hadlee was one of the bowlers, but because I didn't give a chance till I was past a hundred, then tightened up, but still played some fine shots. Eddie Hemmings kept tempting me with some well-flighted off-breaks and I hit him into New Road a few times. Somehow I felt relaxed during this innings, even though I was trying hard not to give it away while scoring fast.

So I had faced three great bowlers in a fortnight and had come out with a double hundred, a century and a 94 (plus two ducks!). It was very satisfying, but I had no inhibitions. I was inexperienced, every day was a new, exciting challenge and, although I listened to our senior players when they talked about the great bowlers, I was determined not to be overawed by them. County cricket was a great test for me at such an early age and I couldn't get enough of it then. I knew that I would learn something valuable every day out there in the middle. Although I didn't realise it at the time, it is now obvious that I had an advantage over some of the opposition because they hadn't seen me bat. So their bowlers would put it in areas that suited me, inviting me to drive off the front foot, giving me too much width for the square cut. When I hit my double hundred against Nottinghamshire, Eddie Hemmings kept tempting me with the flighted delivery, because he must have thought I would hole out eventually. I hit him for five sixes as he tried to lure me down the wicket. He dropped me once, off a sharp caught and bowled, but even when I wasn't quite to the pitch of the flighted ball, I still managed to play it with the turn and hit him over the pavilion. In later seasons, Eddie wasn't quite so attacking!

I hit eleven sixes in the next match, at Neath when we beat Glamorgan in a run-chase. One of them was just about the biggest I have yet managed. Whenever we talk about big sixes in the dressing room and I'm asked what was my biggest, I usually settle for the one at Neath when I hit John Steele on to the roof of a swimming pool. Neath is a smallish ground but that went a long way. I remember another six from that game when we were chasing at around seven an over in the second innings. Ezra Moseley bowled one that turned out to be a yard or two shorter than I expected, so I just stood up and carried on with my shot. It went straight back over his head and as it went past Ezra said, 'Shot, boy!' I liked that, and some of Ezra's friends who were watching him bowl thought it was very funny.

The most important thing about Neath is that we won the game. My double hundred and a fast fifty in the second innings were very satisfying, but it was a very flat wicket, and the ball came nicely on to the bat. In my opinion Tim Curtis didn't get the credit he deserved in that match. He scored two unbeaten sixties and in the first innings he unselfishly gave me the strike as we established a new county record for the second wicket. When we were after the runs on the final day, Tim kept his head, manufactured the strike in favour of those who could hit the ball further and played a great anchor role. He is the ideal man to have as partner in those situations, and I don't think he has ever got the credit he deserved for Worcestershire's recent successes. So many think of him as a solid, slow-scoring opener, yet his record in one-day games blows that one out of the water. He is a very good player, not just a back-up batsman.

July was a great month for me. I just missed out on 1000 first-class runs in the month, but I had little idea of such targets. It was more important to me to play well against an Essex attack containing five Test players (Lever, Foster, Pringle, Gooch and Childs), and then to get a hundred against Garth Le Roux on a fast wicket at Hove, followed by a hundred against Gloucestershire on a slow, two-paced New Road wicket, where the ball started to turn. Occasionally I'd jab down just in time and get the toe of the bat to the ball as it crept along the ground. All varied experience, coming to me day after day in different circumstances. I know my team-mates were pretty happy with my efforts so far, a point that was amusingly made by Phil Newport when we played Essex at Southend. Graham Gooch was playing magnificently on the first day and someone shouted out to Phil as he stood at fine leg, 'What do you think of our Graham then? I bet you wish you had him on your side.' Quick as a flash, Newps turned round and said, 'No, our Graeme's better.' The noisy supporters in the hospitality tents enjoyed that – so did I, because I was fielding not far away and heard the exchange.

The days just seemed to fly past me in that 1986 season. I'm sure it rained a fair amount, but it never seemed to keep us off the field for too long. I remember pulling Ian Botham square when he made his comeback at Weston after being suspended for two months. He was at least two stone overweight, yet it was fate that he should get a fast hundred when the odds were stacked against him. I didn't know him at all then, but I wasn't going to be intimidated by his reputation, especially as he ambled in off a few paces and bowled a few long-hops. He wasn't going to get away with that at this pace, and I enjoyed putting him away. When we played Hampshire, Malcolm Marshall did me for another nought as I played forward to one that left me for a regulation nick to the keeper. At Bristol, I added over 150 with Damian D'Oliveira, in which he completely overshadowed me. We got those runs at around six an over and Dolly played a series of short-arm jabs through midwicket that were out of this world. Walsh and Lawrence just couldn't bowl at him – it was a superb display of clean hitting. We were big pals by then, talking things through if either of us had a moan to air. We tend to have the same sort of views on cricket and we live through each other's emotions. I was delighted for him that day at Bristol, as he got his career-best score and looked a top batsman in the process.

By the time we got to our last championship match, the statisticians were having a field day. I got 61 in the first innings against Glamorgan, which left me needing another 103 to become the youngest in cricket history to get 2000 first-class runs in a season. Poor Hugh Morris was on the end of a declaration that went wrong for him (the same thing happened to him against us two years later at Abergavenny) and we got the runs with just a few balls to spare. As we neared the target it became pretty obvious that we were going to win, and then it was a case of working out who would reach a personal landmark – myself or Phil Neale. The captain had started his innings needing around 80 to get his 1000 first-class runs for the season, something he prided himself on having achieved for a good few years now. With about eight overs to go and about fifty runs needed, I said to Phil, 'Only one of us is going to do it, skip,' and he was a little disappointed at missing out. I got the runs, reached the landmark of 2000 runs and Phil was left just a few short. But I had no option; it was important to win, I was playing well and the loose deliveries came to me. The team's needs came first, but I can't deny I was happy to break Len Hutton's record when the opportunity was there in the last session of the season's last game.

That night, as we celebrated, I had a revealing conversation with Basil D'Oliveira. It was just a short chat, but it meant something to me. In those first few years, Bas hadn't said all that much to me, just a word or two here and there. A few rumours had gone around the club, suggesting that Bas and I didn't get on all that well, because he seemed to spend more of his time encouraging other young players. So as he sat on his own in the Executive Suite on that final night of the season, I said to him, 'Bas, for some reason people think we don't get on. Will you please let me buy you a drink and take it, even if you don't want it?' With that I sat down beside him, we had a little chat and he managed to squeeze out a 'Well played.' That meant more to me than heaps of praise from other areas at the club. Bas knew how to make you earn his respect.

So I'd made cricket history at the age of twenty. It took a long time to sink in, but the achievements of 1986 did make me more confident. It was the first summer I had played exclusively for Worcester and I was enjoying the social life around the city and, if I am honest, I didn't mind the recognition either from the public. By now, Steve Rhodes and I were sharing a house and we'd go into wine bars or pubs and enjoy chatting to our supporters. I was also very useful for Steve because I could spot which girls were in the bar that night – Steve is so short he hasn't got much chance of spotting anybody in a crowded room unless they're standing right beside him! In our serious moments at home, we'd talk cricket for hours. We have the same attitude to the game – we love it, we believe in hard, disciplined work in our profession and we would daydream about pulling on England sweaters in the same team. It would be nice to see that come true.

So my world was an exceptionally pleasant place at the age of twenty. Surmounting fresh cricket challenges, having a few laughs away from the ground with my team-mates, playing a lot of golf – what could be more enjoyable? I was still very green about cricket and its traditions. I was honoured to be named one of Wisden's Five Cricketers of the Year, but I didn't realise that the likes of Mike Gatting, Martin Crowe and Richard Hadlee wouldn't be part of the group. You only get the nomination once in a career, so that took a little of the gloss off it for me. At the dinner in London, I was completely out of my depth. I hardly recognised any of the cricket writers or the administrators from Lord's who were at the dinner. I sat beside Gubby Allen, who was about eighty-five at the time. I had heard of him, but knew little about him or the cricket of his era and he was surprised that I hadn't heard of those he pointed out to me at the dinner. Gubby Allen seemed to think I was ignorant, but I wasn't aware that recognising old players was part of my job. At twenty years of age, I didn't think I was expected to recognise Trevor Bailey or John Woodcock.

At the end of the 1986 season, I remember feeling surprised that so much emphasis had been placed on my getting 2000 runs. I thought that that was a very attainable target and I didn't want to think that I'd never get there again in my career. Perhaps the standard of batting around the country had been deteriorating over a period of time, but 2000 runs isn't a lot when you have around forty innings available. I was really pleased at my new record, but others made me more aware of it than I had been. Perhaps my standards were higher than English players of my own age; certainly I was very hungry at twenty and wanted to succeed. Maybe others weren't as prepared as me to knuckle down to learning as fast as possible. As far as I am concerned, 2000 runs is the minimum you should aim for if you bat in the first four of a county side and don't suffer injuries or serious loss of form.

Even then, I knew that I had made a rod for my own back for future seasons, because much more would now be expected of me. But it was still all a great adventure and I wasn't bothered about self-imposed pressure like that. What I now wanted was to see our side make that final leap from being a good unit with a lot of talent into one that wins trophies. We had lost two more semi-finals in 1986, to make it three successive losing semi-finals in one-day competitions. We were just falling short – perhaps we needed more big-match experience. In the Nat-West game, the toss gave Sussex victory as we were bowled out for just over a hundred on a damp pitch. In the Benson and Hedges semi-final against Kent, Phil Neale and I were building a useful partnership, when he was run out by a smart piece of work by Chris Cowdrey. Then I was out lbw as I tried to dab the ball into the covers to get the strike for the next over. It was awful sitting there as the game dragged to a finish, thinking about the errors that had lost us the chance of playing at Lord's in the final. We just needed that missing ingredient to bring out the best in our young, talented side.

CHAPTER EIGHT

1987: The Breakthrough Season

THE Refuge Assurance League trophy may not be the most glamorous of those on offer to the counties, but there is no doubt in my mind that winning it in 1987 gave Worcestershire a great psychological boost. It also set us up for two more successful seasons, in which we won the championship twice, the Refuge Sunday League again and appeared in a final at Lord's. That first trophy in 1987 gave us breathing space to keep our supporters happy and taught us how to win things. Getting into the habit of winning trophies is a lot harder than developing a losing habit, but it's something you can't teach – you have to go through the experience to feel its value.

We shall never know if Worcestershire would have become such a good side if the club hadn't signed Ian Botham and Graham Dilley before the 1987 season. Perhaps we might have got there eventually, but I'm sure their big-match experience and positive attitude to cricket helped push us along the road that bit quicker. I must admit I wasn't too keen when I heard that Ian had signed for us. I was out in Zimbabwe at the time and my initial thought was 'We don't need him, we're good enough as it is.' I couldn't judge him properly as a player because when I had first played against him the summer before at Weston he was overweight and rusty following a two-month lay-off. Even though I respected his amazing achievements, I was also a little worried about it all turning into a media circus, with the press chasing us for all sorts of trivia. I talked it over with Dad and he felt from his trips to Worcester that we all had old heads on our shoulders even though many of us were still young. He said we wouldn't be led astray down the rocky road by Botham because we were a strong-minded bunch who really cared about our cricket. I knew that our chairman Duncan Fearnley would be all for it, because it would bring glamour to New Road, but he wouldn't have to be with Botham every day on the county circuit. Yet we needed class replacements for Dipak Patel, who had emigrated to New Zealand, and David Smith, who had returned south for business and family reasons. I could see the logic in getting big-name players who were used to winning, who could make things happen in a tight corner.

I was even less sure about Graham Dilley when I heard he had been signed up as well. On the couple of occasions when we had played Kent, Dilley had seemed very unhappy and clearly lacked motivation. I didn't want that kind of player in the team, no matter how good a bowler.

Yet their personalities seemed to change when they came to Worcester and we haven't had any real problems with either Ian or Graham. They have missed a lot of matches through injury and occasional Test calls, but they have turned games for us and we have all learned a lot from them – not least in their attitude that a game is there to be won, that you don't rely on the opposition to give it to you. Graham's ability to get the best batsmen out with late swing has been very valuable; he has knocked over the top order for us time and again when his dodgy knees have allowed him on to the field. As for Ian – the way he drove us on to that first Refuge League title was impressive. He was determined that we would win a trophy in that first season and he never stopped telling us we'd win the Sunday League, even after a bad start. He batted superbly as an opener in the run-in, took vital wickets and never faltered in his belief that we'd win the last two games to clinch the title. That sort of confidence is very contagious when you've come so close to winning things in previous seasons. Somehow we all started to learn things from each other and the other players blossomed under the inspiration of Botham and Dilley. They also proved themselves genuine team men, as pleased about the success of others in the side as about their own achievements.

Graham was very useful in the dressing room in those first

few weeks as we all got used to the two stars. His dry humour was just right for the situation. It helped that both men didn't want to share the limelight, and Graham would just sit quietly in the corner, guffawing at Ian and pulling his leg. On the first day of pre-season training, Ian turned up in a flash raincoat that would have looked better on Joan Collins. It was a real rock-star job and a few of us exchanged sidelong glances as if to say, 'What have we got here then?' I don't know if he was showing off or not, but within a few days he was getting a lot of stick for wearing gear like that, and he took it well. Graham was the perfect foil for Ian because he'd let him make all the noise and do all the wisecracks – then just deflate him with a dry comment as he puffed on his cigarette in the corner. Early on, only older players like Phil Neale, Paul Pridgeon and Graham would take him on, but soon everyone was climbing into Ian and he enjoyed it. I think he knew a bit of give-and-take was needed at a new club and he had enough common sense and respect for our cricketing abilities to stop short of big ego trips. Ian also respected Basil D'Oliveira and would take strong words from him.

We also had to come to terms with the fact that as established, world-class players, Ian and Graham wouldn't net as much as the rest. That didn't bother us, even though most of us are great believers in hard practice, especially pre-season. They did their fair share of that before the serious stuff started and we were quite happy with their involvement. We were all there to make up a cricket team and we knew that Botham and Dilley had their own ways of preparing for matches. On the field they gave us full commitment. It was interesting to see how the atmosphere around New Road changed. The full houses on Sunday contributed a lot to our enjoyment in winning the league, and even on a championship day in midweek you'd get a crowd of around a thousand instead of the usual hundred. On days when you might feel subconsciously sluggish in front of a small crowd, you'd walk out and see people at all corners of the ground and you'd get a buzz out of that. There was a noticeable air that things were going to happen to us as a side in the near future.

The increased media interest worked in our favour too, because it would then be clear that we had other good players, as well as Botham and Dilley, and we'd be happy with the extra publicity. They might not have known all that much about Curtis, Rhodes, Illingworth and Newport, but within a year or two they were either playing for England or going on England tours. It was nice to be the glamour side, to hear about membership rising so fast. We noticed that our sponsors were staying longer with the club. We felt we were in a different league – there always seemed to be someone pouring pink champagne at the ground that year, and the players didn't mind that one little bit! Our captain, Phil Neale, had always said that Botham and Dilley would be no problem to handle and he was right. Phil didn't make a fuss about them, he knew that we were all good pros who wouldn't alter our lifestyles just because Ian Botham was a team-mate, and that we all wanted to make our own mark on cricket as well.

It was an interesting experience batting with Ian on Sundays. The experiment of getting him in as opener on Sundays worked because he would invariably start us off on an aggressive footing and we'd take it from there. I didn't realise until I batted with him just how far down the wicket he comes when he's launching himself into the straight drive. Because he hits it so hard, I had to work out where to stand because he wasn't all that far away from me once he connected with the ball. We only had one major stand that summer, when we beat Essex in the Sunday League by nine wickets and Both went mad, smashing an unbeaten hundred. We'd all been out with the Essex boys the night before at a country pub, where Ian's great friend Eric Clapton had entertained us with some brilliant guitar playing. Ian had promised the Essex bowlers he was going to give them a hammering the next day, and he did. Early on he was dropped off a skier and he laughed down the wicket at me and said, 'The wheel of fortune's changed – here goes.' He just smashed them all over the place.

We got on a roll in August in the Sunday League and clocked up five wins out of the last six games. In the last game, against Northants, we knew from a long way out that we were going

to beat them and take the title. That was a brilliant feeling –
savouring the atmosphere, anticipating the champagne, hearing our
supporters going berserk. I was out there at the end, as we won by
nine wickets, and as we threw champagne over each other in the
dressing room afterwards, one of the lads said, 'So this is how the
other half lives.' We all wanted more of the same. It was great to go
into the members' bar, looking for my girlfriend Jackie, surrounded
by supporters slapping me and the other lads on the back. It was
particularly satisfying for those of us who had grown up together at
New Road in recent years and to look around that members' bar and
see all the happy faces. Our supporters had been just as frustrated
as us at recent near-misses and you could see that this trophy would
keep them happy during the winter. I was pleased for Phil Neale,
Paul Pridgeon and Basil D'Oliveira because they had seen the lean
times at New Road over a fair number of years. It was all new to
the younger players, but Phil, Paul and Basil remembered what it
was like to win the championship in 1974. That had to be the next
landmark, to prove we were now one of the top three sides in the
country.

We hadn't done as well in the championship as we might –
partly through injuries, Test calls and rain washing us away when
we were in promising positions. I got nearly 1900 first-class runs,
yet many felt I'd played better in the previous season, even though
I got almost 3000 runs in all competitions in 1987. Although I was
happy with the overall volume of runs that year, I do prefer to get
big scores in first-class cricket, and on that basis I did have a bit of
a lean spell on a couple of occasions. Each time Basil D'Oliveira was
a great support to me. Early on I was getting out playing one-day
shots in championship matches. We were playing a lot of one-day
cricket at the time, but I do know the difference in approach and
I couldn't work out why I couldn't settle in the longer games. Basil
wasn't impressed when I was stranded down the pitch at Old Trafford
and stumped off the left-arm spinner Ian Folley. I had just hit Folley
for a straight six, and even though the ball was turning sharply, I
fancied doing it again. I went down the wicket to him, the ball
turned and I was yards out. In the dressing room, Basil said to

me, 'If you're a good enough player, you don't need to leave your crease.' After that, I stuck to my crease for the rest of that season, even when I managed to hit sixes off the spinners. But for a time I still struggled in the championship, and eventually Basil sat me down and simplified things for me. He didn't talk technicalities, he discussed the mental attitude to batting and to dominating bowlers. He said to me, 'What's your job? You're a batsman, so you go out and hit the ball. Don't think about anything else. No theories.' Basil has always admired Tom Graveney and he gave me one of Tom's quotes when he was going through a lean time. Tom said to him, 'Next season, I shall be on my way to another 2000 runs, so I'm not going to bother about this bad patch. I'm just going to think about the hundred I'm going to score next time.' Basil told me to think ahead, to concentrate on future ambitions, rather than dwell on current failures. Tell myself I'm a good player and analyse why – then get back to the style that made me a good batsman, forgetting the little hiccups.

Basil cleared my mind. In the past I have turned to Dad for guidance but this was the first time I had sat down and had a really serious talk with someone else. That was the first time I realised how important it was to unclutter the mind and sort out the mental stresses of the game. Basil made me confident again, reassured me that I had a good technique, that the runs would soon start to come again. He wasn't very impressed by the way I had started to go back and across against the fast bowlers, instead of my usual slight movement forward. I was getting trapped lbw shuffling across my stumps, and chasing wide deliveries to be caught behind. He said, 'Why are you doing that? What's wrong with the method that's got you this far? You've got to play your own natural way.' He was right, of course; I just needed to reassess the way I build an innings.

My parents proved to be a good omen as I snapped out of my bad trot. They arrived in late July, the day before we were due to play Somerset, and they brought me luck. I had decided to keep my pads out of the way as much as possible to avoid the risk of lbw. I opened up my stance a little and played as much as

I could with my bat. I told myself to keep my feet away from the ball early on and then I'd revert to my normal style later. It worked. I grafted away to a hundred and felt very relieved. August proved to be a fruitful month for me. The game after Somerset, I scored 173 on my first championship appearance at Lord's. I had another big stand with Tim Curtis and was slightly annoyed to miss out on a double hundred. The pressure for a declaration and the fact that Phil Neale just couldn't get the ball away at the other end contributed to my dismissal, as I stepped away to try to hit Wayne Daniel through the offside and ended up being bowled.

But I was excited at getting a hundred at Lord's, even though the ground lacked atmosphere for just a county match. Maybe there are grounds in other parts of the world where the facilities are superior, but when you say you got a hundred at Lord's, that seems to carry a bit more stature than Eden Gardens, Calcutta or the Melbourne Cricket Ground. I found the hardest part of batting at Lord's is the slope. You find yourself falling over slightly when batting at the Pavilion End due to the slope and you are a candidate for lbw. When batting at the Nursery End, you can stand up more, but you're conscious that the ball might come back up the slope so you end up playing at more deliveries than perhaps you need. Presumably you get used to it the more you play there. I loved playing at Lord's for the first time and I still get a buzz out of the place. I'm also amused that some say I never get runs at Lord's, presumably basing that on failing in two finals. Yet I got 173 in my first championship match there in 1987 and another 170-odd there in 1988 for Champion County v. the MCC. Perhaps people have selective memories!

My good August run continued when I narrowly missed out on two hundreds in the match at Northampton. I had got to 87, playing fluently, when I chipped an inswinger lazily to midwicket. It should have gone to the midwicket boundary all along the ground and I was very annoyed at myself. In the second innings, we just failed in a run-chase, and the need for runs was so acute that I even got the hook shot out of the bag. I top-edged the intended hook off Winston Davis for six, but I was about as impressed with the shot as the bowler.

77

That championship season almost ended too soon for me, as I cashed in with three more hundreds in the last three games. I was particularly pleased with my century at Colchester against Essex; after surviving an lbw appeal early on that must have been very close, I felt I played very well, with the feet moving in the right place and the bat coming down straight. It was also nice to get a hundred in the Bank Holiday match against our local rivals, Warwickshire. I hadn't forgotten Basil's remark a few years earlier ('This lot don't think you can play') and Basil never misses the chance to remind me of it when the Warwickshire game is coming up.

So I ended up with eight championship hundreds, more than anyone else in the country, but what pleased me most was the way I had come through a lean period when I was thinking negatively and starting to blame things like the wicket. Basil had demonstrated to me what a simple game it really is by talking practical common sense. He had renewed my self-confidence and when I had another bad run in 1989 I had no hesitation in going to him again. He may have been a little remote to me in my early years on the staff, but Basil D'Oliveira was now becoming a valuable, wise guide. With my self-confidence repaired, and Worcestershire at last breaking their trophy duck in the 1980s, I couldn't wait for the next season to see if we could make a genuine challenge for the championship. Our supporters, those genuine ones who know their cricket, would not be happy with just a Sunday League title. We had the squad of players to win the prize that all first-class cricketers in England value the highest. But before then, I had another challenge to face. My cricket education was about to be extended in New Zealand.

CHAPTER NINE

Continuing My Education

As my 1987 English summer drew to a close, I had to make an important decision – where did I want to spend the next few months playing my cricket? Did I want to go back to Zimbabwe or stretch myself somewhere else in the world? It was time to get extra experience and Dad was instrumental in getting me to New Zealand to play club and first-class cricket for Northern Districts. A couple of years earlier he had taken out a team to the Hamilton area, which is right in the middle of North Island, and he had loved the trip. Mum also went on the tour and they both came back raving about the friendliness of the locals and the beauty of the country. They said the cricket wasn't bad either! Over a drink one night Dad happened to mention to them that his son wasn't a bad player and said he hoped I might go out there one day and play some cricket. Then I got a letter during the 1987 English season from John Turkington, the executive officer of Northern Districts Cricket Association: would I like to go out there and play for them?

My parents were very enthusiastic and the three of us felt that the experience of playing first-class cricket would do me some good. It would be the first Christmas I would spend away from the family, but that has to happen some time. From a cricketing point of view, it made sense because if I went to visit the folks back home I wouldn't be stretched by another season in Zimbabwean club cricket and, now that I had opted out of the national side, that was all I could expect to play in Harare. I knew that I needed to improve my knowledge of batsmanship, to get used to different challenges on wickets in other parts of the world. I knew that New Zealand wickets are generally slow and low, with the ball not coming on to the bat as it does in Zimbabwe, but that is something a batsman has to face: if I was serious about qualifying for England, then I had to find out about pitches other than those in Zimbabwe and England. I was perfectly aware that a lot of luck was needed if I was ever going to attract the attention of England's selectors, but if I did manage to force my way in eventually by sheer weight of runs in a few years, I felt that the fact that I was willing to play in other countries wouldn't count against me. A batsman with ambitions to play in the highest company can't pick and choose where he learns his trade – he has to diversify as much as possible. I also felt the New Zealand trip would be good for me on a personal level; it would do me good to go somewhere new, to make new friends and integrate myself into a different way of life.

As soon as I got to Hamilton, I was struck by the warmth of the welcome, and the similarity to Zimbabwe. It was just as spacious with a great deal of natural contrasting beauty. The pace of life suited me – things could always be put off till tomorrow – and everyone seemed dedicated to the outdoor life. I spent a lot of time early on with John Turkington in his office at the Northern Districts ground and my digs were just three hundred yards from the front entrance to the ground. A lot of folk remembered Dad from his tour and I soon felt at home. I was struck by the importance of rugby as soon as I got to Hamilton – when I first talked to the press, they said I was built like a rugby player and wanted to know if I had ever played the game and what was my position. They thought I'd make a good second-row forward, but I told them I was a lineout specialist because I had a bit of pace as well! In the first press reports about me, the local cricket writers all remarked on how I would make a good rugby player – I was rather keener on just being a good cricketer, but it brought home to me that rugby is almost a religion out there, compared to cricket.

The outdoor life of New Zealand was ideal for me. Lovely beaches, plenty of barbecues and lots of free time to play golf. I liked the fact that we had some free time between matches, and it was up to each player how he prepared himself for the matches. In my case I started to work very hard in a gym in Hamilton (up to two hours a day) and then I joined an aerobics class to improve my mobility. Those aerobics classes definitely loosened me up and eventually I could touch my toes, to my great delight. Everyone seemed so fitness-conscious out there; in my aerobics class, the membership was split between the sexes and many massive rugby players would be working out alongside slender ladies to get fit for their new season.

Fitness training over there seemed as natural as having breakfast. You could be driving home and see so many people out running that by the time you had parked your car, you'd feel compelled to get out and do the same. I had always been keen on gym work since working out in Ian Robertson's gym in Harare, but the one in Hamilton was magnificent, with so many facilities. Aerobics classes were going on from 6.30 in the morning, almost like a school timetable, and I'd plan my free days around the time I could get into the gym or an aerobics class. The work I put in there definitely helped me as a cricketer. All those records I set up a few months later in England owed something to my increased stamina and flexibility, because I didn't get out all that often in the sixties or seventies: I had found the reserves to get me through to a long innings.

Although I turned in impressive figures in that first season with Northern Districts, I was a little disappointed with my lack of consistency. The first month proved typical. In the club games I started well with a double hundred, but then got a few low scores as well. The standard of club cricket wasn't as high as in Zimbabwe, where the country's best players all clash against each other; in Hamilton, a hundred was there for the taking because you could rely on two loose balls an over. It was also disconcerting playing alongside another set of cricketers in an adjoining match. The cricket grounds were so massive that they could accommodate two matches at the same time, with boundaries overlapping. One day, fielding on the square-leg boundary, I kept having to look behind me in case someone smashed a ball in my direction: I quickly asked the skipper if I could field nearer the bat!

After the initial club games, I started off the first-class season equally erratically, with three noughts and two hundreds. I wasn't playing too well in my opinion, even though everyone was so kind and full of praise for me. I was trying too hard and the hundreds came when we were looking to set up a target for the opposition in the fourth innings. I would have preferred to score my hundreds in the first innings, rather than the second. I also didn't back up the hundreds with a few half-centuries; noughts then hundreds isn't my usual pattern of scoring, it's too unpredictable. By the time Mike Gatting's England team had arrived in New Zealand to play a Test series, I was a little tense because I wanted to do well against them when they played Northern Districts. I knew that all the English cricket correspondents would be there, that they'd be writing about me, and comparing me to the current group of batsmen in Gatting's side. I needed to relax before that match, so I took myself off for a couple of days with a team-mate, David White. We packed a tee-shirt, a pair of shorts and sandals each and headed for Mount Maunganui, a lovely spot about an hour's drive away. We had a terrific time, surf-boarding and fooling around on a catamaran and I felt really refreshed when I got back, ready for the England game.

I made only 19 in the first innings, and although I was annoyed at the way I got out – a leading edge from one that I had tried to flick over midwicket from Neil Foster – I was encouraged by the way I batted. A couple of straight drives and a square cut told me that my feet were at last moving properly and I felt confident for the first time that trip. I was playing straight again, not looking to work the ball square, and the bad habits that had crept in seemed to have gone. In the second innings, I got 146, with a few sixes – mostly off Eddie Hemmings, but the one I really enjoyed went over extra cover from my county colleague, Graham Dilley.

I still pull his leg about that shot, and we still have a laugh about the moment when he was convinced he had me caught behind. I went to pull him, got a faint bottom edge and it went through to Bruce French. They had a big appeal, it was given not out and Graham paused in his follow-through and asked if I had hit it. I told him that I had, but that the ball had not carried to Bruce; I had swung round after I'd played the pull shot and I definitely saw it bounce before the keeper took it. Besides, I had already passed my hundred, so it wasn't as if I was desperate for runs, so I would have walked if I thought it had been legitimately caught. I was given not out and Dill wasn't too impressed. He was even less happy next ball when I hit him for six. It was a flat, humming six and I carried on running down to Dill's end as I watched the ball disappear. I tapped my bat in the crease after looping around the bowler, smiled at him and ran back as he swore loudly at me. I keep telling him it's a batsman's game! The English press made a lot of my innings, but I think the best knock came from Tim Robinson as he won it for England with a great, attacking effort in the run chase. All I had done was set up the target, but I was pleased with my performance and after that I played better for the rest of the season.

I finished up scoring more runs than anyone else in first-class cricket that season, averaging 63, with four hundreds. The fact that everyone at Northern Districts was so pleased and excited for me was very touching, but I knew within myself that I ought to have done better. Perhaps I was too relaxed, too aware that on the slow wickets no one was going to come along and threaten to knock my head off – as I had come to expect in England, with the likes of Marshall, Walsh and Clarke around. All the top Kiwi players were unavailable because they were touring with the national side, so the standard inevitably dropped in their absence. By now I had got used to daily pressure in England, looking forward to batting against a star bowler, relishing the challenge.

I felt that if I had got my runs at a more crucial stage in the games, then Northern Districts would have won the Shell Shield for only the third time. We finished just short of the winners, Otago, and the difference was only the amount of first innings points that they had won. In New Zealand, a lot of emphasis is placed on first-innings points and they ended up with sixteen to our twelve. We had won our first three Shell Shield matches, but the fact that we had trailed each time on first innings counted against us. In the fourth, against Central Districts, the game was affected by rain and high winds which blew down the press box – this at a stage when we were almost certain to pick up at least valuable first-innings points.

It seemed to me that the Northern Districts players were more concerned about putting one over on their bitter rivals, Auckland, than the wider issues like winning the Shield. Since Auckland broke away from Northern Districts in the 1950s there has always been an edge in the games, and when I was there they kept saying to me, 'We've just got to beat the Aucks.' The big three were Otago, Auckland and Canterbury, and perhaps there was a subconscious feeling among Northern Districts players that they lacked the depth to win the Shield consistently, so that beating Auckland was enough to get them through a season. I was amazed that when I got a hundred in a limited-overs match it was the first time ever from a Northern Districts player. That just proved that they had lacked a strong group of players in their short history.

So I felt frustrated that I just couldn't help to get us over that hump to win the Shield. Apart from that, the most important thing for me was the greater experience that New Zealand gave me, both this season and the following one. It was a different form of first-class cricket and I had to adapt to the slow pitches that favoured only the seamers, who looked to pitch it on a length and keep it tight. I had to graft away, not expecting to be able to stand up and crash the ball through extra cover off the back foot. Patience became very important. I had to tell myself that if I just stayed in, the loose ones would come along. When I batted against Michael Holding at Lancaster Park, even he was reduced by the conditions to bowling line and length off a Sunday League run-up and trying to move it off the seam. I even managed to hit him straight back over his head for six in that innings, something I would never have expected to do at Derby or Chesterfield!

With so many top players away, I couldn't really gauge the true standard of New Zealand cricket in that first season. Chris Cairns looked as if he could be a very good all-rounder when I first saw him. A new-ball bowler, he also has a lot of talent with the bat and could easily bat at seven in an English county side. Since then, he has struggled with a back injury and I'm not sure now just how desperate he is for success. He had to contend with a lot of publicity early on, because his father had been a famous Test player, and he

One of my favourite shots of myself at the crease. I seem to have got most things right here.

With my parents and dog (Cricket) at Trelawney, the tobacco farm that Dad runs and where I grew up.

These pictures were taken on the school playing fields by the Banket First Eleven coach, Rob Altschul. I was eleven at the time – glad to see I was keeping my head down even then!

Aged fifteen, in the Prince Edward School First Eleven. I am in the front row on the right; Eddo Brandes, currently in the Zimbabwean national side, is fourth from the left in the back row. The white blazer shows you have won your cricket colours.

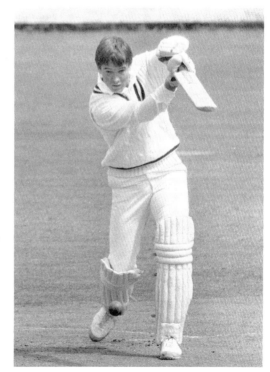

My first innings in England, May 1983. I was playing for Zimbabwe against a Birmingham League side at the Mitchell and Butlers ground, Birmingham. I seem to remember scoring a half-century on a damp pitch.

Savouring the moment when I got to a thousand runs by the end of May, at Worcester in 1988. My parents flew in that day to see me – Mum was there on the balcony steps to congratulate me. Dad is in the dark glasses just behind me as I walk off the field.

(*Above and opposite*) Another landmark – the century for Champion County against MCC at Lord's in April 1989. I ended up with 173 not out.

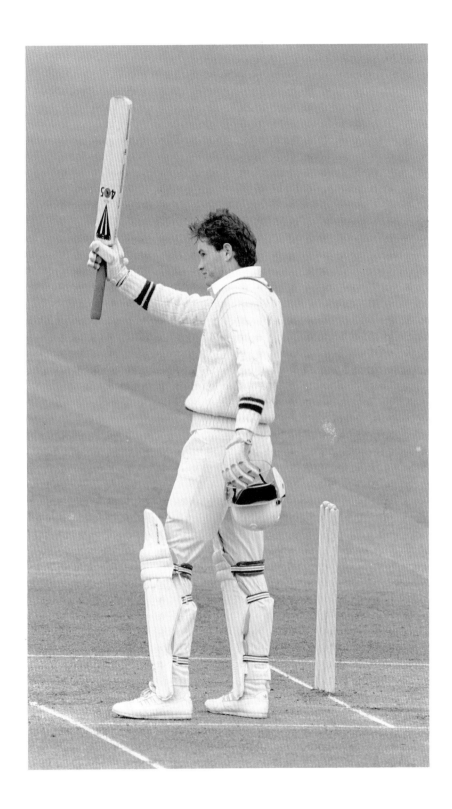

In action against Middlesex, July 1990.

sometimes seemed keener on enjoying the social aspects of cricket than on the hard work, but the natural talent is there. His father, Lance, was very good value when he captained Northern Districts in one-day games. He would run in and bowl fast leg-breaks, then hit the ball miles. He and I shared a century partnership in one game in about fifty minutes and on a wicket that was slow and damp, he kept planting the ball over the midwicket boundary. Lance is from a farming family and is apparently deaf in one ear; as a result, he was a fairly quiet guy – but when he stood at the bar, fuelled by a couple of beers, he was very funny and great company. I wish he had played in the Shield games as well, because I am sure I would have learned a lot from him.

I think the New Zealand umpires could learn from their English counterparts about facing up to the players and imposing their authority on the game. That was my biggest reservation about cricket in New Zealand. It wasn't that the umpiring standard was blatantly inferior to that in England – more that they allowed the players to hassle them and often buckled in the end. The players simply weren't disciplined enough to accept the umpire's decision and get on with the game, and I'm afraid I got sucked into it as well. Of course, there were some bad decisions, but they even themselves out over a period of time and, in any case, a bad decision can work in your favour. Yet it got to the stage where players would appeal for everything and just wear the umpires down. Far too often, they'd openly laugh at an umpire and they'd push it to the very limit. Some of the umpires were gibbering wrecks eventually, after putting up with an afternoon of bad language thrown at them and general dissent and disrespect.

At the start of my first season with Northern Districts, I made my feelings known to my team-mates that I would continue walking if I knew I was out, and they couldn't believe it. I only suffered one bad decision in that season; I had no bat/pad decisions go against me – they are often the dodgy ones – yet I got dragged down after a time. I'd find myself appealing for things that I knew weren't out on the basis that the more you appeal, the luckier you'll get. Every other side was doing it and there was no point in expecting sportsmanship to be rewarded. It was dog-eat-dog and I felt sorry for the umpires, who were being placed in an impossible position by the relentless gamesmanship. In England, players would never be allowed to get away with it.

Apart from that one cricketing reservation, I loved my first summer in New Zealand. I made friendships that will last, and some of my new pals have come over to stay with me at Worcester, where we natter away about old times. Last summer, my surfing mate David White rang me up at nearly midnight from New Zealand to say that he had been picked for the national side's tour to Pakistan; I was absolutely delighted for him. I know that whenever I am in Australia and have a few days to spare, I'll hop over to North Island, hire a car and drive to Hamilton, where I'll be welcomed warmly. I had expected to have bouts of homesickness, yet the friendship I encountered in Hamilton was a great help. Even Christmas Day passed happily; I had been building up to my first Christmas away from my family for a couple of weeks, but then John Turkington suggested I fly my girlfriend Jackie over from Worcester. We got it organised within a couple of days and we spent Christmas Day with Paul Pridgeon and his family in Auckland. With Steve Rhodes also joining us (he was playing club cricket out there), it was a Worcestershire reunion and a great day.

The trip did me a lot of good as a cricketer as well. Although I felt I ought to have batted better, my technique held up in conditions that were unusual to me. It was good for me to be in the field for long periods. Because of the emphasis on first-innings points, it would often be a case of churning out big totals on slow pitches that gave the bowler no chance. Then you would have to be patient and work out ways to dismiss batsmen. We bowled 192 overs against Auckland and 193 in the Otago game, spending almost two days in the field each time. That sort of hard experience is good for a young cricketer who wants fresh experiences; it makes you think about your game.

When I returned to Worcester in the spring of 1988, I was a better cricketer for the New Zealand experience. I was also a fitter cricketer and that was more relevant to my achievements that May than any technical experience I had picked up with Northern Districts. I had reached a peak of stamina and muscular flexibility, and that was to prove invaluable over the next few months.

CHAPTER TEN

A Thousand Runs in May

'M not the kind of person who thinks that a notable achievement can't be repeated, but if I have to settle for a memorable season it would be the 1988 summer with Worcestershire. In the space of a few months, I made the highest score in English first-class cricket this century, became only the second batsman since the war to score a thousand first-class runs by the end of May and saw my county win the championship, the Refuge Assurance League and appear in two cup finals. Worcestershire proved to be the team of the season and with a bit of luck we would have won more trophies; our team success meant a great deal to me and we did it despite Test calls and Ian Botham's serious back injury, which put him out for almost the entire season. It was a triumph for team spirit and although many suggested that my achievements made us a one-man team I will never have that. Bowlers win you championships and ours did us proud. Everyone chipped in at some vital time with a significant contribution, but I was the one who seemed to grab all the headlines. I just accepted that – after all, it's nice to get media attention when you're playing well and setting up records – but I never lost sight of the fact that the needs of the side were more important than building up large personal scores.

The confidence and the extra fitness I brought back from New Zealand gave me a great start in April, when so many county cricketers are just feeling their way into the season. I began with a double hundred against Lancashire, then my 405 not out against Somerset gave another boost to my confidence. I never thought I batted badly during the 1988 summer, even though there wasn't a lot you could do about some of the dismissals on the New Road wickets. Without a doubt, they were testing for batsmen, but my success in May gave me the confidence not to drag my lip about getting unplayable deliveries at various times in the season. The runs also kept coming in the Sunday League, so I always looked forward to the next game, telling myself I would make runs. I felt sorry for some of my team-mates who seemed to get more difficult deliveries than I did, and we could see how it affected their confidence when we played away from home. The opposition batsmen would show by their footwork and general approach at the crease that they had been scoring runs and were looking in good nick, while the Worcestershire boys seemed instinctively to be waiting for the ball to leap up off a length. That was the legacy from playing at New Road, where the pitches that season were erratic in bounce. If I hadn't enjoyed such a good start away from home on good batting pitches, I might have struggled as well. I certainly did at the start of the following season.

The introduction of four-day cricket that summer helped both me and Worcestershire. We had a balanced attack and the longer game suited us because, when the pitch started to turn later in the game, Richard Illingworth would come into his own. As for me, I was happy just to go out and bat for long periods without taking any undue risks. I managed to score my runs pretty quickly and that gave us even more time to bowl out the opposition twice. You can't expect to win many four-day matches on a run-chase and we won five of the six games of that duration in 1988 by taking twenty wickets each time. Getting a good start to the season was vital and we won all three of our four-day games that started the experiment towards longer matches. By the end of the third game – against Somerset – I had scored 815 runs in first-class cricket that season and it was only 9 May, so you can rightly assume I was a big fan of the four-day game!

Although my 405 not out at Taunton has dominated many people's thoughts about my 1988 season, I was just as pleased with my 212 against Lancashire a couple of weeks earlier. The Old Trafford pitch was a bigger test than the flat one at Taunton and the ball turned sharply on the first morning. I had little experience of batting on a wicket that helped the spinners, so I set my stall out to play everything from the crease – I hadn't forgotten Basil D'Oliveira's stern words the year before when I had been stumped by yards at Old Trafford. The ball beat the bat a lot but I didn't let it bother me. Anyone can bowl a good ball but as long as you don't get out to it, why worry? I felt I batted clinically and tightly, punishing the bad ball, making sure I didn't commit myself too soon in case it turned a lot.

I seemed to be able to pick up the line of the ball quickly that day, although I think Ian Folley might have been tighter with his slow left-arm spin. He was perhaps trying to turn it too much and when he dragged the ball down now and again, I was on to the cut as he dropped it short to me. I think Jack Simmons might have bowled just outside off-stump at me, rather than straight, because I could then play a lot of his straight deliveries with the pad, knowing that the off-spin would drift the ball down legside. If he had aimed a little more to the offside, I might have struggled due to the fact that I couldn't pad him away for fear of an lbw decision. I wasn't complaining about that, though; it was up to them to work that one out. I was pleased that the next top score in the match was 68 and that we won the game by ten wickets. The ball must have been turning though, because I picked up four wickets in their second innings! Even though their spinners might have made it harder for us on a wicket that definitely favoured them, I was still very pleased at that innings. It remains one of the best I have played.

I played very freely in the next championship match, against Nottinghamshire, with 86 not out before lunch on the first day. Then I was caught at slip in the first over after the break. They did bowl loosely, though – short and wide, with 72 of my runs coming in boundaries. It must have been a good bat! I had been using one that served me well in New Zealand and it kept going until midway through the season. So the bat that got me to a thousand runs before the end of May eventually found its way back to my bat maker, Duncan Fearnley, who hung it in his showroom. Fair enough; he did a good job on that bat!

Again my score was the highest in the match and, after beating

Nottinghamshire by six wickets, morale in the team was high. We had beaten last year's champions and another fancied side in the first two games and we saw no reason why Somerset wouldn't be the third to go down. They did – by an innings – but not until I had made history and discovered who Archie MacLaren was. If you had asked me about him before 6 May 1988, I wouldn't have had a clue. It turned out that he had played for Lancashire and England at the turn of the century and that he had made the highest score in first-class cricket in England, way back in 1895 – at Taunton: there's a coincidence. I finally heard about MacLaren and his 424 during the tea interval on the second day against Somerset, as I sat there trying to digest the fact that I had just scored 405 not out. How I got to that total will remain very clear in my mind.

I had never really got runs before at Taunton, for some reason. It had been a good wicket whenever I had played there and they weren't the strongest bowling side, so I couldn't put my finger on the explanation. I checked into our hotel on the Wednesday night after sitting around for two whole days watching the rain come down at Old Hill, where we had been trying to start the Benson and Hedges Cup match against the Minor Counties. We never did get on the field and it was with some relief that we heard the weather was going to pick up.

Phil Neale won the toss on a perfect day for batting, with sunshine and a nice breeze and the crowd in shirtsleeves. The wicket was ideal for me – true, with little bounce but at least regular bounce, so you wouldn't get trapped by one that scuttled through at ankle height. After Gordon Lord and Tim Curtis had given us a solid start, I came in about forty-five minutes before lunch. I got off the mark first ball when I tucked one away just in front of square leg. I read afterwards that their captain Peter Roebuck had thought about putting a man there, but had decided against it; if he had, I might easily have been out because I hit the ball in the air, although only at shin height. You always need a bit of luck. I got to lunch on 31 not out and all seemed plain sailing. But then we had a clatter of wickets, with Ian Botham yorked and Phil Neale and Damian D'Oliveira caught by ones that moved away sharply.

So I had to forget all ideas about smashing it around and, with the score 132 for 5, it was simply a case of batting for security.

Just over twenty-four hours later, we declared at 628 for 7, and great credit for that must go to my three partners, Steve Rhodes, Phil Newport and Richard Illingworth. Peter Roebuck made the point afterwards that he was impressed by the fact that I had never hesitated about running my partners' runs, that they seemed just as important to me as if they were off my own bat. Well, that seems obvious to me. I don't score runs for me, I score them for the team and I like to think that I'd be as supportive as my partners that day in Taunton if someone was playing a lot of strokes at the other end.

Steve Rhodes stayed with me for the rest of that first day and he supported me superbly. He was happy just to stay there, not playing his usual aggressive game, but running very quickly between the wickets and giving me a fair amount of the strike. We were worried about getting rolled over on the first day, then having to field for two days and getting bowled out on the last day. Occupation of the crease was the first objective. By tea, I had got to 103 not out, playing within myself and enjoying a little bit of luck. On 67, I had played a bad shot to a ball slightly wide, got a nick and saw Martin Crowe dive to his right at second slip and get a finger to the ball. Then on 101, I had pulled one in front of square, just through the fingertips of midwicket. By the close, we were back in the game at 312 for 5 and I was 179 not out. I didn't feel tired, even though I'd batted for five hours; I was pleased with my form and looking forward to batting for at least another session. I liked this four-day cricket: no need to rush headlong into your shots!

That evening, most of us went to an Indian restaurant and Gordon Lord joked about me getting 300. I didn't think much about that – I was just going to bat as long as I could. It was interesting that eight of my ten first-class hundreds that season came after an Indian meal – perhaps I should have a few more curries when my scores are low! On the Friday morning, I felt refreshed and ready to capitalise on the previous day's recovery. I asked our captain, Phil Neale, what he wanted and he said, 'Bat through this session and, if we can, we'll go on till teatime. Then I might declare.' I was happy with that; it was a four-day game after all, the weather was now settled and we knew that Martin Crowe would be looking to play a big innings. We wanted a large enough total to make them realise that they'd have to bat for an awful long time to avoid defeat. Steve Rhodes kept me company for a while on that second morning and then Newps and Illy were just as sensible. There wasn't a great deal in the wicket and, when they took the second new ball, I found it came nicely on to the bat.

It all went according to plan and at lunch I was 257 not out. I had passed my career-best in first-class cricket by then (230 for Zimbabwe against Glamorgan), and I wasn't at all keyed up when I came off at lunch. I'm never one to sit on my own throughout an interval if I'm not out. I like to have a natter and a laugh with the lads around the lunch table so I joined them for half an hour. I felt pretty good – you do when you're 257 not out! Just before I went out, Duncan Fearnley put another thought in my mind. 'Don't forget Glenn Turner's 311 not out,' he said. That was the highest Worcestershire score in their first-class history and I made a mental note of that. My own personal target was 311, to get past my highest score in all cricket – that 310 against Ireland in 1986. Phil Neale said, 'Just keep on batting,' and he reminded me that he'd probably want to declare at tea.

Somerset kept trying throughout my innings. The only time they flagged was when Roebuck came on to bowl a few floaters late on, but he wasn't on just to give me runs – I still had to work for them. I got to my triple hundred with a couple of sixes off Graham Rose over long-off and then quickly went past 311 to post a new record for myself and Worcestershire. I remember looking up at the clock, saw it was twenty-five minutes to four and thought, 'No need to hold back now, if it's there I'll go for it.' It seemed to work out pretty well! I never slogged at any time. I went down the wicket and hit the seamers straight for a few sixes, and Vic Marks went for a couple over long-on. I was aware that the crowd was growing every few minutes as word obviously spread through the town that I was advancing on 400 and that got the adrenalin going. I was now really in the mood, I felt so positive, and Richard Illingworth was very pumped up as well. Taunton's like Worcester in terms of atmosphere and a few thousand can make a good sound. I rather like the short straight boundaries at Taunton as well!

It seemed I was on the verge of the 400 in next to no time. Illy and I were still running the singles for each other, even though I did lose the strike sometimes. The final over before tea from Colin Dredge is very clear in my memory. I went from 393 to 399 with a six over midwicket, then another in that over went the same way to post the 400. I managed to get hold of a picture of umpire Roy Palmer signalling that second six with me turning round, grinning from ear to ear, and I remember feeling absolutely delighted as Illy pumped my hand. I can just picture him when he's eighty, going on about cricket like a typical Yorkshireman, telling his grandchildren about the part he played in that historic day! He was very genuine in his congratulations, as were the Somerset players. As they shook my hand, it dawned on me that Phil Neale had declared, so we walked off. Then I realised that there was still one ball to go before tea. Later in the bar I asked Phil why he had declared and he said it was because he hadn't wanted me to get out off the last ball. I half-jokingly said I would have liked to have gone for a third successive six, but I wasn't particularly upset. Nor was I all that bothered that he didn't give me a couple of overs after tea to beat MacLaren's record. Many cricket fans love to see records tumble but the interests of the team must always come first; it made sense to see if we could get some quick wickets against a tired Somerset side before close of play.

When I came through the backslapping of my team-mates on the Worcestershire balcony, I had a quick shower and did a couple of TV interviews. That was no hardship. If you can't take the attentions of the media after you've scored 405 not out, then you will never do so. It was absolutely typical that I'd then come on and bowl after tea and take two wickets. It was my day and I was fated to be the Golden Arm that night. The ball was turning and by the time Nigel Felton had hit me straight to mid-off and Richard Harden had planted his front leg in front of a straight one, I was laughing my head off! That night, I really enjoyed my time with the Worcester lads; no one really knew me in Taunton so I could start taking it in quietly with no hassle from strangers and well-wishers. The boys were really pleased for me, rightly feeling that they'd shared in my success and occasionally one of them would just look at me and say quietly, 'Bloody hell, Hicky, what have you done?' Duncan Fearnley had rung up my family within half an hour of the declaration, and Mike, my brother-in-law, thought Duncan had said the team had scored 405. 'What did Graeme get?' he asked and couldn't believe it when he was told that that was my score. I managed to talk to Mum and Dad for five minutes on the Sunday morning – then Jackie took the phone off me and seemed to talk for a good deal longer than that! On that Friday night I had a quiet smile to myself as my head hit the pillow and I bought all the papers for the next few days – and not just because Dad keeps a scrapbook back in Zimbabwe.

Not surprisingly Somerset were a little demoralised after the first couple of days and we won by an innings. I felt sorry for Phil Newport that his ten wickets in the match didn't get wider acknowledgement, because he bowled really well, moving it around off a full length. There wasn't a great deal in the pitch and, even though they were tired, Somerset could have batted out for a draw if Newps hadn't bowled so effectively. So to win the game was a perfect conclusion to a few happy days down in Taunton.

Of course I remember vividly the six off Colin Dredge that got me past 400 but the other two that really stick are the ones off Graham Rose that saw me to the triple century. I obtained a video of the innings and on the soundtrack you can hear a couple of old spectators cackling away, and passing a few comments about the bowling as the ball soared into the crowd both times. Dad has that video at home now – I must look at it again some time. Vic Marks also received some punishment from me, but he never lost his sense of humour. The following year, after he hit me for six in a Sunday League game, he found himself at my end and said, 'I reckon you still owe me another thirty of them for last year' – accompanied by that lovely infectious Vic Marks chuckle.

I suppose it wasn't until I drove home to Worcester on the

Monday that the full impact of that innings sank in. I was tired by then; adrenalin and excitement had kept me going for the previous few days, but now I was pretty whacked. The papers didn't let go of the story for several days afterwards, so I had time to think about the historical significance of it all, to reflect on the fact that the fitness training in New Zealand had much to do with being able to bat for so long, and to keep running sharp singles right to the final over. The media asked me if I thought I'd get to 400 again and I have to be honest and tell myself that I can. It's like having an amazing round of golf – it can happen and you must tell yourself that it's within your capabilities if you've already done it once. Whether I do it is a different thing, and I would be thrilled if it were to happen, but I won't close the door on such a possibility. If it happens for Worcestershire, and Phil Neale is still the captain, I have a sneaking feeling that he might not declare until I'd had a crack at Archie MacLaren's record. He took some stick for declaring when he did, but I don't blame him for that. The captain has to think about the needs of his side at all times.

So now all the talk was about getting a thousand runs before the end of May. Only Glenn Turner had done it since the war and everybody seemed to think it was a formality now for me, with six possible innings left and 185 runs needed. I thought that would be a nice landmark to get, definitely one of the more worthwhile batting records, but after the next two matches I thought I had blown my chances. Against Somerset in the return game I made 8 and 11 – 386 less than at Taunton – and at Leicester, 6 and 7. Somerset's Adrian Jones had me caught twice in the gully and for the next couple of seasons pulled my leg about being his rabbit. At Leicester, on a green pitch with plenty of movement, I was bowled twice.

That was that as far as the media were concerned, especially as my last chance was against the West Indies, the best bowling side in the world. Strangely enough, I felt totally relaxed after the Leicester match because no one was putting pressure on me any more. You don't get many 150s against the West Indies, especially on a New Road pitch and with several of their fast bowlers looking for a place in the Test side for the following week at Trent Bridge.

It was still lurking away in the back of my mind, though. A long shot, but there was always a chance. I was keyed up about playing them for the experience alone, having played against them all as individuals but not as a team. The night before the game, I went to a benefit function for Phil Neale in a pub near Evesham and felt totally relaxed about the challenge ahead. I didn't get home until after midnight – no Indian meal this time – and slept very well. It was mainly out of my hands now, so why worry all that much? I was just looking forward to the challenge of batting against the West Indies.

It was fate that we only played one full day's cricket in the next three days and that I was only going to get one chance. Luckily it happened on the first day, when the weather was fine and it was also lucky that I had all day to get the runs because Gordon Lord was yorked by Curtley Ambrose in the first over. I walked in, needing 153 for the target and my parents just about to land at Heathrow. They were always coming over at that time – nothing to do with this latest challenge – but it was fate that saw them get to the ground just before lunch, when I was not out 30-odd. I had a quick look for them at lunch, but couldn't find them. I understand they spent the afternoon circling the ground with Jackie, too tense to watch my progress.

I remember thinking at lunchtime that it had been the longest session I had batted for so few runs and it was a really testing period of play that I thoroughly enjoyed. It was a lively wicket and I was lucky a couple of times when the ball gloved me and looped over the head of Gus Logie at short leg, into vacant spaces. They thought that I had nicked one to the wicket-keeper when I had scored 17, but I stood my ground, convinced I hadn't touched it. Ian Bishop had bowled me one of full length that I tried to dig out, but missed as I hit the ground with my bat. They all appealed and were rather annoyed when the appeal went my way. I honestly can say that I would have walked if I had touched it, even though my chance of getting the thousand runs would then have more or less disappeared.

I was convinced I hadn't nicked it, yet for a few overs afterwards

I heard comments like 'Keep going, we'll get him again.' Later on, when Tim Curtis and I started to play more freely, there were more comments that sounded a little like sour grapes and I was surprised at them. A side of their calibre doesn't need to indulge in that kind of chat; they were far superior to us, but didn't want to accept the umpire's decision on that one appeal. When I reached the landmark, only about four of them on the field said 'Well done' to me, but I wasn't bothered about that. I like to think that I'd have enough respect for a guy who has done well to congratulate him – even now if someone has reached fifty or a hundred, I'll give him a clap even if he hasn't played all that well. It is recognition for a professional achievement, no matter how lucky the batsman has been. The ball was a very full delivery and it deflected a long way off the wicket but I hadn't got anywhere near it. If it had been a county game, nobody would have thought any more about the decision, but as no further wicket fell all day, they got more and more uptight and frustrated. But I didn't let it bother me, I just batted.

After weathering the initial hostility from Patterson and Ambrose, I felt more comfortable. When they realised they weren't going to run through us, they throttled back. Walsh and Bishop also tried hard for the first few overs when they came on, but eventually all four of them stopped going flat out. I was surprised that Viv Richards used the off-spin of himself and Carl Hooper for as long as he did, and that certainly made it easier for Tim Curtis and myself. Tim was absolutely rock solid and a great man to have in such a situation. Basil D'Oliveira said afterwards he was sure that I'd get to 153 but, if Tim had got out, I'm not so sure. We didn't discuss the landmark ahead, it was just a batting partnership, but I've always enjoyed batting with Tim and he was tremendous support for me that day.

We looked at each other in surprise when it dawned on us that Richards and Hooper were staying on after I had got to my hundred. That was a slightly worrying time for me, because now I didn't want to get out for less than 153. I could have handled it if I had gone cheaply, but not now. We worked it out that there were bound to be some bad deliveries from Richards and Hooper and hoped they would get me through to 140-odd before I had to start fending the ball off from in front of my face again. That's exactly what happened as we played comparatively freely for a time. Then Ambrose came back around 5.30. I needed another six runs. By now I could see in Tim's face how anxious he was. At the end of each over, I could sense the strain in him as we talked. Perhaps he was worried about running me out! The hard work at this stage was just waiting for the bad ball, staying in the positive frame of mind that would mean I could punish it when it finally came along.

It all happened in one over from Ambrose: first a four through square leg, then, with two needed, a square cut that hit the fence just in front of the members' bar. I can still see everyone standing in the crowd to applaud me as the ball hit that fence. The crowd had grown over the last couple of hours and, just as in Taunton, that helped lift me.

That night I did the decent thing and treated Tim Curtis and his wife to dinner, along with Duncan Fearnley and his wife and my parents. I felt I owed one to my bat maker and my reliable batting partner! It was ironic that my parents had arrived the previous year when I had gone through a bad patch only to see me score a hundred the day after they arrived – and now, within hours of their arrival from Zimbabwe, I was scoring the crucial runs. I felt very tired that night, but exhilarated. I knew I had only reached the landmark because of one major innings, but apart from Taunton, the wickets hadn't favoured batting and I had worked hard for those runs. You play on so many bad wickets that you have to cash in when a good one like Taunton appears in the fixture list.

I am often asked which of the two performances means more to me – the 405 not out, or the thousand runs before the end of May. I suppose the runs have been scored by other batsmen in this century, but not the quadruple hundred, so perhaps the 405 means more. Yet getting the crucial runs against the West Indies gave me great satisfaction and I was annoyed that I got out the next morning to Patterson's loosener for 172, without adding to my overnight score. I would have loved to get a double hundred against the West Indies, something that rarely happens, but I was rather embarrassed when everyone stood to applaud me as I walked off. After all, I had made nought that morning, yet there I was, acknowledging the applause. For all that, I was very happy at the achievement and having my parents there to see it meant such a lot to me.

Cricket is the great leveller, though. Down to earth in the next first-class match with scores of 0 and 8 against Lancashire as nineteen wickets fell in the day at New Road. The Test and County Cricket Board (TCCB) had allowed counties to experiment with pitch preparation that season in order to get pace and bounce into the wickets. At Worcester the Cricket Committee asked the Head Groundsman to leave a little more grass on the pitch and to roll this into the surface during preparation. It certainly produced some pace, but it also gave us some awkward variable bounce. The TCCB's Inspector of Pitches was called in to examine the surface and some of our batters were struggling with their confidence. I sympathised and thanked my lucky stars that my record in May would give me consolation if I kept falling to balls that just cleaned me up, with nothing I could do. Whenever I played and missed, I told myself not to worry, because that might be the fault of the pitch, rather than because of any bowling skill. What annoyed most were the times when my concentration lapsed and I got myself out. That happened several times in the summer of 1988 when I seemed to see the ball so well, so early. Against Derbyshire I was really annoyed to get out for 47 against the bowling of Bruce Roberts, who used to get me to clean his boots back at Prince Edward's all those years ago. I thought I'd climb into him and soon I was thinking about another hundred. That's one of the danger times, when the concentration goes and you're soon back in the pavilion. I missed out on double hundreds against Hampshire (when they didn't have a very strong attack and time was available to me), against Yorkshire (when I chipped carelessly to square leg), and against Glamorgan (when I hit one very hard, but low to deep midwicket). Each time I ended up with big scores (177, 198 and 197), but they might have been even larger if I had kept concentrating.

An innings that gave me a lot of pleasure that year in the championship wasn't even a hundred, it was 78 at Lord's on a green wicket against Middlesex when we were both jostling for the lead at the top of the table. Cowans, Williams, Fraser and Hughes were a handful that day as the ball darted around and we failed to get maximum bonus points. Tim Curtis anchored the innings in his usual style, I played and missed at a few, didn't let it worry me and hit some good boundaries. After a forfeit on a couple of innings, Phil Newport took eight wickets and we bowled them out cheaply to win an important game. I was happy that in the context of a low-scoring game, my 78 had been important.

The luckiest hundred for me that season came against Northants, when I was dropped three times, two of them very easy chances. I thought, 'I'm obviously meant to get a hundred here,' and so it was. The biggest thrill for me in that match was batting against Dennis Lillee. At the time, he was thirty-nine, with nothing to prove, but he still showed what a marvellous bowler he had been. I wasn't sure what pace he would be bowling, and every now and then he'd slip in a faster one that moved sharply away. A couple of times I hit him for boundaries when he clearly thought he had bowled a good delivery and I could tell by his look that I wouldn't have got away with it a few years earlier. Although I was feeling good at the crease, I knew that on his day Lillee would have seen me off fairly comfortably. I was simply pleased to have played just once against one of the greats.

By the middle of August, the championship seemed to rest between ourselves, Essex and Kent. Kent had surprised many – including some of their supporters, judging by the comments we picked up when we played them at Folkestone. Many expected their bubble to burst, but they kept on fielding superbly under Chris Cowdrey's aggressive captaincy. We still felt we were the better side though, and that was confirmed in our minds when we had the better of the drawn championship game and beat them by seven wickets in the Refuge League that same weekend down at Folkestone. By now, we were looking a good all-round side, with big wins over Sussex, Hampshire and Middlesex and a narrow win in the rain when Yorkshire sportingly kept going for victory. Snatching wins like that one tends to convince you that it could be your year. Yet Kent kept on our tails and by the time we came to Abergavenny in mid-August we knew that we had to beat Glamorgan and keep on in the same vein for the next month. The side that finished the strongest would win the title.

In the end, we beat Glamorgan by five wickets with four balls to spare after I had scored 159. Yet it wasn't a one-man show. We needed almost 350 at five an over and you can't get that against first-class cricketers unless at least two of you are firing for a long time. Again it was Tim Curtis who played the sensible innings to anchor our charge while I fired off the shots at the other end. Tim seems to be able to work out the runs and overs equation quicker than the rest of us and he soon made me realise that as well as quick singles, we needed a boundary every over as well. It was a good batting wicket on a smallish ground and all the bowlers could hope to do on that final afternoon was to bowl straight and put us under pressure in the hope of inducing some mistakes. The run-rate crept up to around eight an over from a long way out, but we finally managed to get going and I lost three balls with straight sixes. I was out near the end – caught beside the sightscreen – and we still weren't home. Martin Weston, with a couple of big sixes, and Phil Neale saw us there for an important win against the odds. We now felt we were on a roll, that teams who win the title win games like the Abergavenny one. Yet it was still to be a hard month before we could celebrate.

From Abergavenny we had to travel down to the Oval in south London for the next day's match against Surrey. It took hours by car and at one stage the M25 motorway was so packed that we came off and had a few beers in a pub while we waited for the traffic to subside. I had developed cramp after batting so long in the heat at Abergavenny and I felt exhausted when we finally got to our hotel at 12.30, hardly the ideal preparation for such an important match. People who look at the remaining fixtures and try to assess who will be champions often forget the effect that that kind of travelling can have on a side. It can be a killer on the road during the August school holidays and you need luck with your fixtures if you're looking to win the title. On that first day at the Oval I went in to bat feeling very dozy. A ball early on from Mark Feltham soon woke me up as it hit me on the jawbone!

I was a lot sharper in the second innings when I hit the fastest hundred of the season. When we came off at lunch, Damian D'Oliveira asked our scorer Jim Sewter how many balls were needed if I had a chance. He told me I had to get another 23 off twelve balls and with that Dolly sat up top in the pavilion, gesturing to show how many balls I had left. Ian Greig, the Surrey captain, gave us nothing throughout the match and he certainly wasn't going to make it easy for me at this stage. Finally, Chris Bullen came on and bowled one that swung in at my legs. I just flicked at it, hoping it would go for a one-bounce four and I was amazed to see the ball sail over the boundary. I couldn't believe it, as I stared at my bat, wondering why I couldn't time the ball so well all the time! Next ball, I sneaked a couple of runs and I was there in 79 balls, with one delivery to spare.

Unfortunately that was the only highlight of that game for us as rain washed out any chance of a definite result and we were even more disappointed in the next match when Essex beat us on a New Road pitch that deteriorated the longer the game went on. We lost it in the first session, when Graham Gooch took advantage of some loose bowling. After that, things were pretty even but Essex were such a good, hard side that they weren't going to let us off the hook. So they were now back in contention for the title with just three games to go. We worked out that we had to win at least two of them and when rain, then some solid Warwickshire batting, led to a draw in the local derby, the situation became even more clearcut. Wins over Gloucestershire and Glamorgan were vital, preferably with the maximum of 24 points each time.

At Bristol, I got a hundred on the first day and one from Phil Neale saw us past 400, even though we couldn't get the full batting bonus points. That was because the ball was turning sharply even on the first day and David Graveney tested us out. I have always thought him a very underrated spinner – he's tall, and therefore gets bounce, he is accurate and has subtle little variations. He eventually bowled me off my pads with a slightly quicker one, not the first time that Grav has got the better of me. With the ball turning, we needed to set them a big score in the final innings and Gordon Lord came good at the right time. He scored a vital hundred as Grav took six more wickets. The ball must have turned because I got five wickets in the match, and ended up sharing sixty-seven overs with Richard Illingworth in their final innings. In the end we bowled them out after some resistance and breathed a little easier. Thank heavens for four-day cricket – it gave us the chance to build a big lead without worrying too much about the weather.

We were even more pleased when we learned that Kent could only draw with Middlesex. That meant that even if they beat Surrey in their last game, we would be champions, provided we beat Glamorgan – and picked up the maximum points. When Surrey collapsed from 100 for 2 to 109 all out on the second day (a deficit of 250), we knew that our destiny lay in our hands. Kent were going to win and we had to do the same, picking up four points each for bowling and batting. We had got the bowling ones easily enough on the first day, but the batting ones on another interesting New Road pitch were a harder proposition. I played well to get to a hundred, but then we had a mini-collapse to find us 263/5, with the target of 300 still a fair way adrift. Steve Rhodes, an ideal man for such a situation, came in to join me and for a time we only scored around two and a half an over. We knew we had to get it up to four an over if we were to reach 300 inside 100 overs and Greg Thomas didn't make it easy for us with some very fast overs. I just moved out of the way of one very rapid delivery and at the end of the over Steve said, 'Well played,' but that was only because I had been in for a long time and was seeing the ball well. In the end we got the runs with seventeen balls to spare and then built up a large lead before close of play. So we had another two days left to bowl out Glamorgan again and, despite a delayed start on the third day because someone had vandalised part of the wicket, we got there just after tea with more than a day to spare.

It was a brilliant feeling when David Leatherdale caught the last man, because we had had time to savour the excitement as wickets kept falling at regular intervals. The home spectators also increase your pleasure; it wouldn't have been the same to win the championship somewhere else, then climb into your car and drive back to Worcester. It was a great moment for us all to stand there on the players' balcony, waving to friends and supporters as the champagne was sprayed all over us.

I was pleased for so many of my colleagues that day. Basil D'Oliveira had had much to do with the development of many of the young players standing on that balcony and he had been in the team the last time Worcestershire won the championship in 1974. Phil Neale had just joined the club back in those days and his contribution had been immense in 1988. He had batted very well – getting his hundreds at vital times – led the team well, coped with the strains of his benefit year, and above all lived with the fact that his son Craig had contracted leukaemia earlier in the year. One day earlier in the season, Phil closed the dressing-room door and told us about Craig. He said his contribution to our season hinged completely on Craig's health: if he had a relapse he would just have to sit out the games. Luckily Craig seemed to rally during the season and Phil kept in touch with developments when we played away. It must have been a terrific strain on him, but he's the type who needs to keep going, to fidget over all sorts of things, so perhaps the responsibilities of captaincy kept him sane that summer, instead of worrying every moment over Craig. Whatever the background it was a great effort by Phil. We had also coped with the loss of Ian Botham from early in May with his back injury. Judging by his contributions in 1987, Beefy had been set for a good season and we missed him on and off the field. But after a wobble or two soon after he dropped out, we got by with increased commitment from everyone.

There were several turning points in our charge to the title. That win against the clock at Abergavenny was vital. Getting five wins out of six in the four-day games underlined our all-round abilities. It's so important to get a good start because you can then build up your momentum. It's no use hoping for a late run in August and September because the weather can let you down. You have to try to make the running early and that's what we did. We made things happen. We needed to win those last two matches and we did. We needed full batting points against Glamorgan and we got them. That 197 was one of my most important innings for Worcestershire and it gave me great satisfaction to get us past the 300 target in time, then go on and pile up a big lead. It was a pressure innings on a pitch that was far from easy and Steve Rhodes's contribution mustn't be forgotten either.

Far too many people were of the opinion that it was a one-man effort for Worcestershire that season. Even though I was obviously delighted with 3500 runs in all competitions, I can't forget the performances put in by my team-mates. In 1988, Tim Curtis, Neal Radford, Graham Dilley and Phil Newport all played for England, while Steve Rhodes was picked for the tour to India that was abandoned for political reasons. Martin Weston did very well as substitute all-rounder for Ian Botham, while Richard Illingworth had his best season so far. At some stage in the season, each of us made a telling contribution and all I did was get runs comparatively quickly, to give us time to bowl out the opposition twice.

We were the team of the summer and with a bit more luck we might just have won all five competitions on offer. We lost in the quarter-finals of the Benson and Hedges Cup to the eventual winners, Hampshire, solely due to a magnificent innings by Robin Smith after we had been bowled out for 169 on a very difficult New Road wicket. You needed luck to survive very long on it and even though Robin was dropped a couple of times, all credit to him for a terrific, matchwinning knock. We won the Refuge Assurance League again, taking 38 points out of the last 40. Tim Curtis and I both scored over 500 runs and once again the team that gets on a roll has a great chance, because towards the end of the season some sides lack motivation if they are nowhere in the race for the title or prize money. After losing the first two matches that season, we only lost one more and we cruised home by beating Warwickshire by ten wickets in the final game. We were then in the final of the Refuge Cup, a new competition staged at Edgbaston, and Lancashire were the more motivated side. We didn't play at all well, feeling a little jaded after winning the championship two days earlier. Lancashire fully deserved to win the final, but I know that Phil Neale was disappointed that we didn't do ourselves justice.

Our biggest disappointment was losing the Nat-West final by three wickets to Middlesex. In common with the rest of the lads, I was really excited about appearing in a final at Lord's and we all felt let down that losing the toss was so decisive. It is true there had been a lot of rain recently, but when we were put in by Mike Gatting, conditions for batting before lunch were very tricky. It wasn't a fair contest because most people agree that a satisfactory one-day wicket should favour the bat, yet on that damp morning we faced forty-two balls without getting a run. I was one of the batsmen involved at the time and I had to work hard to stay in. We just didn't get a bad ball from Angus Fraser and Norman Cowans until I finally broke the deadlock with a four through the covers.

I felt better after that, but then I was bowled by one from Fraser that came back up the hill, went over the knee roll of my pad and hit the top of middle and off. I couldn't do much about that delivery, but it left us at 9 for 3. Phil Neale, David Leatherdale and Martin Weston bravely got us up to 161 for 9 in our sixty overs and when we had them 25/4, then 65/5, we were in with a great chance, with Graham Dilley bowling superbly. We might have won it if I had caught Mark Ramprakash at slip, with about thirty runs needed. I got a finger to it as I stood wide, allowing Steve Rhodes the chance of covering a larger distance than usual. In the end Ramprakash won it for them with a dashing innings, full of attractive shots but also risky ones. He could have been out at any time as he chanced his arm and it was a typical young player's innings, with no inhibitions. Yet if he had got himself out, Middlesex would have said he had lost them the game through playing unnecessary, flamboyant shots.

Yet we gave it our best shot and didn't disgrace ourselves. I enjoyed the occasion very much indeed, even though I was sorry I made so few runs. The game had been built up in the media as a contest between myself and Mike Gatting, yet we only made four runs between us. So the myth started that I never make runs at Lord's, and fail on the big occasion. As for Lord's, those with short memories will have forgotten my 173 the previous season and my 78 three months earlier against Middlesex. As for the big occasion, I did fail, due to a good delivery from a fine bowler in conditions that favoured him. I would have thought that I had shown what I could do on numerous other big occasions as we surged towards the championship or towards a thousand runs by the end of May – but some folk want their story and they won't be budged. Failure in the 1988 Nat-West Final wasn't going to cause me too many sleepless nights once I had watched the dismissal several times on the video and felt sure that good bowling, rather than loose batting, had been the cause.

By the middle of September, we were all pretty tired. We had kept going for five months and although it's always easier when you're running on the adrenalin of success, the end of the season was welcome. It had been a great season for me on a personal level as well as a team member. I had been an important part of the country's best side, kept the statisticians – and myself – happy with my batting performances, and had enjoyed the atmosphere and challenge of facing up to the West Indies at the end of May. All over the country, cricketers were brandishing new Duncan Fearnley bats with the '405' logo on the back, sweatshirts with the same motif were appearing at every ground and people kept coming up to me to say that they had been there at Taunton on the famous day. The Taunton ground must hold more people than I thought! I didn't realise it at the time, but my achievements in 1988 were to make things a little more difficult for me from now on. If I was to emulate that season again, few would be surprised, while if I fall short of it, some would be bound to say, 'What's gone wrong with Graeme Hick?' At the age of twenty-two, I had set myself a ridiculously high standard; it was on my record from now on. Since 1988, I have put in some performances which have really pleased me but which have rarely raised a ripple elsewhere because it was now expected of me. I have had to learn that a certain amount of eminence in sport also leads to a few detractors wondering what all the fuss is about.

CHAPTER ELEVEN

More Records in New Zealand

THANKFULLY I hadn't used up all my good fortune after our championship season because I carried on scoring runs a few months later in New Zealand, where I spent a second enjoyable season with Northern Districts. In first-class games, I averaged almost a hundred and my six centuries were a record for Northern Districts. That made it ten for them in two seasons and I was surprised that that was also a new record for the club. It may have been going for just thirty-odd years, but there have been some fine batsmen wearing the ND colours and it's not as if the wickets are anything other than slow and fairly flat as a rule, or the bowling all that penetrative. Any batsman is happy to set new records, though, and I was just glad that I seemed to get the hang of the pitches quicker than the previous season, so that I played with confidence throughout that second summer on North Island. There would have been something wrong with my psychological make-up if I hadn't brought a lot of self-confidence with me after my satisfying season with Worcestershire, and I felt I played to the standards I was now demanding of myself.

Unfortunately, we just couldn't manage to win the Shell Shield after again going so close. We were leading the table when the final round of games began. We had a great chance to beat Canterbury, who hadn't yet won a game that season – they were 4 for 4 on the final morning, but then we dropped a vital catch. Poor Chris Kuggeleijn, our captain, dropped Mark Priest in the slips before he had scored; that would have made it 5 for 5, but then Priest and Rod Latham added more than 250 for that wicket. They set us 376 at around five and a half an over, a steep challenge considering that the wicket wasn't all that trustworthy, but we were going for it. Our wicket-keeper, Bryan Young was promoted to open with David White and they smashed a hundred for the first wicket in no time at all. After that, it was more or less a Sunday League target, but we kept losing wickets at the wrong time. I got in, started to play my shots and then got a leading edge as I tried to chip a leg-spinner over midwicket, to be caught for 41 as Stu Roberts ran twenty-five yards to take a good, tumbling catch. So we fell 62 short. We could console ourselves that we had given it a real crack, but once we had lost five wickets, we knew it was all over. To make it worse, Auckland won the Shield for the first time in eight years – the 'Aucks', our fierce rivals. This after beating them in our two Shield games that season.

That first match against Auckland turned out to be the first time I had ever been involved in any unpleasantness on the field. It came about because the Test off-spinner John Bracewell kept needling me. I had heard that he had a reputation for being a fairly fiery customer, and that he wasn't slow to express his opinions to a batsman who was getting the better of him, and that he could make it hard work for the umpires if he felt like it. Well, on this day, he was in his most truculent mood. I had come in with Northern Districts needing well over 300 to get a surprise victory over Auckland. There seemed little chance of that after we had been outplayed for two and a half days and they were walking around as if they didn't think we deserved to be on the same field as them. They did have some good players but our lads had grown up disliking the superior attitude the 'Aucks' always showed to Northern Districts. We were determined to avoid defeat at least that day, and if we could beat them on a run-chase, terrific. It would be our first-ever defeat of the 'Aucks' in first-class cricket.

By tea, I was 38 not out, having suffered the rare indignity of getting the slow handclap from the crowd. But I wanted us to consolidate after losing three early wickets and then decided to go for it, because I didn't think they'd have time to bowl us out if we lost more wickets in the chase. When Bracewell came on to bowl, I went down the pitch to try to hit him through the covers for four, but I missed it. I expected to hear the wicket-keeper stumping me, and then saw the ball going out to square leg. So I took the single as Bracewell stood there, cursing his luck, and the keeper looking a little downcast.

Before that, we had had words when Bracewell had tried to run me out from slip. Danny Morrison had been appealing a lot for lbw as the ball kept slanting in at the pads and, after one such appeal, the ball slid to the slips. I stood on my crease in the half-and-half position, with my back foot well inside, when Bracewell threw down the stumps from slip and had a huge appeal. He had been niggling the umpires for quite some time, pushing his luck, and when he moaned loudly at the umpire quite rightly ruling in my favour, I had had enough. I told him where to put himself because he was making such a fuss and he shouted, 'You might think you own Zimbabwe, but you don't own New Zealand.' Normally I wouldn't ever get involved in something so petty but I'd had enough and replied, 'I've never claimed to own Zimbabwe and I wouldn't want to own New Zealand.' All very silly but I didn't feel I should take any more and I felt sorry for the umpires.

So when Bracewell had missed out on the chance of getting me stumped, his humour didn't improve. I then played my first reverse sweep in first-class cricket and I knew that that would rile him even more. Unfortunately the fielder who had to chase after the ball as it neared the boundary was Trevor Franklin. Now Trevor was making his way back into first-class cricket after a freak accident at Heathrow Airport in 1986 when a baggage trolley had clattered into him and gave him a broken leg that was far from a clean break. So he wasn't the quickest man to chase after the ball in the Auckland side and Bracewell stood there, fuming. Then Trevor dived at the ball as it neared the boundary and half his body and his legs went over the rope. Obviously I hoped he hadn't hurt himself, but when I saw him standing on the rope, I assumed the umpire would signal four, as is the usual custom. I politely enquired of the umpire, 'Is that four?', to avoid having to run a fourth run, and Bracewell overheard me and shouted, 'You get on with your batting, the umpires are here to decide that.' I thought that that was a bit much considering the way he had handled the umpires, but I decided to stay out of it after that. Even when he needled me with, 'What the hell are you doing in this country?' I didn't take the bait. My captain, Chris Kuggeleijn told me, 'See him off, that's the only way to shut him up,' so I did just that. I took 35 off him in the next two overs and we ended up winning. I got 211 not out and Shane Thomson backed me up superbly, playing like Tim Curtis – and I mean that as high praise. Shane ran the singles at the right time and when the field was set back, he would occasionally chance his arm and find the boundary. We ended up winning by five wickets and the 'Aucks' weren't at all happy.

After that game, Bracewell had another go at me in his weekly newspaper column, saying that I shouldn't be allowed to play in New Zealand, that overseas players weren't the best thing for home cricket. He also said we were lucky to win, because they had had much the better of the match. That's true, but that's cricket. I refused to get involved in a slanging match, preferring to let the public read Bracewell's moans and let them draw their own conclusions. It only served to fire us up for the return match soon after, and we won that as well, chasing 60-odd in poor light with just a few overs available. We got them for the loss of just two wickets in nine overs. I got a quick 30 as Danny Morrison bounced four or five an over at me; he hit me in the solar plexus with one of them and I went down like a sack of potatoes. That required desperate remedies – so I got the hook shot out of the bag. Definitely a last-resort stroke for me! So we went past Auckland in the table and fancied our chances for the rest of the season, but then teams changed their attitude to us. They started to take us seriously and set stiff declarations. Rain ruined our match against Central Districts when we were in a good position, and when we came to the last match – the one against Canterbury – the fates were stacked against us.

Incidentally, John Bracewell didn't play in the return match for some reason. I don't know if he still bears a grudge against me, but I hope not. When the New Zealanders played at Worcester a year later, we said 'Hello' to each other, and that was more or less that. He's entitled to his opinion about overseas players occupying places in New Zealand cricket, but I obviously wouldn't agree with him. That game at Auckland was the only time I have ever been involved in any kind of aggro on the field, and I don't want a repeat of it. I usually say very little to anyone when I'm out there in any case. I'll talk to someone and have a quick cheery word if he starts up a conversation, but I don't like to lose my concentration by chatting too much. A word with my batting partner at the end of an over is more than enough for me.

I reached another personal landmark in that New Zealand summer – two hundreds in a first-class match for the first time. I had come close at Northampton in 1987 and it was something I had fancied doing, so when the Wellington bowlers came to Morrinville, a tiny town on North Island, I was delighted to manage it. I was also pleased at the way I batted, because it wasn't an easy wicket (a little two-paced with the odd one really taking off), and I had to work for all my runs in the first innings, and the first 70-odd in the next innings, before they threw up some easy stuff to encourage a declaration. I wasn't bothered about that – the runs were in the book. Getting two centuries in a match is always a bit problematical because of the state of the game, the pitch and the quality of the bowling, but it's a worthwhile aim for any batsman. It boosts the average as well! There are plenty of times when your sum total from two innings doesn't get into double figures.

Away from the cricket field, one of the most demanding moments for me was making my debut as a public speaker. That is something I am not used to even now, and when the Cambridge Cricket Association asked me to come and talk to them over dinner, I was in a panic. I thought, 'What on earth am I going to talk about?' I still say the same when I am asked to go through with it again. The organisers told me that they just wanted me to talk, so I said I'd speak for ten minutes, then I'd take questions from the floor: I reckoned they wouldn't be so bored with me if they could get involved. So I came out with a few stories (quite a lot about Ian Botham, surprisingly enough!), and to my amazement I was on my feet for twenty minutes. As I waffled on, Jackie sat there nervously throwing glances up at me, knowing that this wasn't my favourite activity. Then we started the question-and-answer session and the first one was 'Who's the best all-rounder, Ian Botham or Richard Hadlee?' I diplomatically said that Ian's Test record was still superior to Richard's at that time, but they were both great players, and I seemed to get away with that. The next question was even more direct – 'Who's the better batsman, you or Martin Crowe?' Both questioners had put them to me with a grin on their face, as if to say they knew they were putting me on the spot with a daft question, so each time I had to think quickly. I said that Martin was obviously a superior batsman to me, because he had played Test cricket and done well and that seemed to satisfy them.

All in all it was an evening that contributed to my cricket education. Since then I've done quite a few question-and-answer sessions and I enjoy them, because I can speak naturally and honestly while remaining diplomatic. I prefer them to standing on my feet for far too long, waffling away and boring myself as well as the audience. Perhaps in a few years I'll be better at speechifying when I have greater personal experience of the game and can talk with authority and practical knowledge about things that particularly concern me.

During that stay in New Zealand, I had both an inkling that my qualification period for England might be cut, then a scare story that it was to be extended. In December 1988, Mike Vockins wrote to me from Worcester telling me that there was a proposal at Lord's that the period be cut from ten years to five for those from Associate Member countries in the International Cricket Conference. In other words I might be eligible to play against Australia in the 1989 season, a fact I discovered with some excitement when I looked up the forthcoming tours to England. Mike did warn me that the vote might go against the proposal, though, so I wasn't disappointed when he wrote again and said it had. I had set my sights on ten years. There was never any chance of my doing a Dipak Patel and getting a fairly quick qualification for New Zealand. England it was for me and I would wait. Then, in March 1989, Mike wrote with some exciting news. The Test and County Cricket Board at Lord's had approved a recommendation from its registration committee, reducing the qualifying period from ten years to seven. So I would be eligible for England from 31 March 1991 rather than three years later. Mike told me there was no chance of a reversal, that it was now 1991. Even when I learned that the West Indies were the tourists that year, I was still excited!

There was a downside to all this. Reporters from England thought it a good idea to keep tumbling me out of bed at one o'clock in the morning to check my reaction to the news. It was a pity they couldn't work out the time difference nor, in some cases, apologise for waking me up. In the end, I pulled the plug out of the wall socket and got uninterrupted sleep. The press chased me around a few weeks later on another registration story, this time one with little foundation. A reporter had delved into my career in Zimbabwe and had discovered that I had played in one first-class game in 1986, in Harare. In other words, the qualification period should then have been seven years from that 1986 game, rather than from my arrival in England in 1984. I remembered the match – it had been against New South Wales in March of that year. They had come out on a replacement trip at short notice because England's tour had been called off. At the time the match had not been deemed of first-class status, but after the tour the Australian Cricket Board said that it was first-class. Mike Vockins reassured me that just because the Australian Cricket Board had reached a particular decision retrospectively it should not affect my eligibility. He said that he had checked out my credentials with Lord's and that, as I had stuck by the book, I had nothing to worry about. I couldn't be held responsible for a match subsequently being elevated to a status it didn't have at the time it was played. I have continued to be meticulous about checking which games I should play in when I go back to Zimbabwe, just in case someone comes up with another scare story. When the England A side toured Zimbabwe early in 1990, Mike Vockins advised me not to play against them. The match against Zimbabwe Country Districts was not a first-class fixture but Mike thought I had come so close that it would be silly to jeopardise my qualification for England by playing against an England side! I accepted that, just as I have every time he has advised me. That's why I wasn't too perturbed when one or two English newspapers suggested that a match in 1986 against New South Wales would affect my availability for England five years later.

I was more perturbed about another complication in my cricket career soon after I got back from New Zealand. A big offer was on its way to play in Australia for Queensland. It proved to be a complex issue that caused me a lot of agonising. It would also affect my form for the first month of the new English season.

CHAPTER TWELVE

Triumph in Adversity

IN some ways the English season of 1989 was more satisfying for me than the year before, when I couldn't stop making runs and Worcestershire had been easily the best side in the country. In 1989, we again won the championship but we all had to fight that much harder for it against the odds – with the result that second time around was so much sweeter. We were troubled by serious injuries all summer. Test calls took away Phil Newport, Ian Botham, Tim Curtis and Graham Dilley for various periods and we had to deal with the home pitches at New Road, which for a second season proved a major problem for our batsmen. After a time, it was clear that we were at a disadvantage playing at home, because the confidence of our batsmen was very low. Batsmen from the opposing side would turn up, some of them in form, and play well even though the wicket was unreliable. We got fatalistic after a month of the 1989 season; the home dressing room was too negative about batting out there. 'Here we go again,' someone would say when the ball started misbehaving, seaming around, keeping low or darting up off a length. Eventually we snapped out of it and put together an impressive run that brought us the championship.

At last I started to play well, but for the first two months I had the worst trot in first-class cricket so far in my career. Looking back on it, I feel mentally stronger for the experience: it was good for me to snap out of my depression, work hard at my mental approach and get back to basics. That 1989 season made me a better player, even though some might say that, by my standards, I didn't have much of a summer. Considering all that was involved,

I was more than happy with a first-class average of 57, six hundreds and more sixes than anyone else in the country. Only Jimmy Cook got more first-class runs and centuries than I did, and Jimmy would be the first to admit that the conditions were a little easier down at Taunton than at Worcester for much of the season.

I started under a cloud and it was partly my fault that I allowed it to affect me for the first few weeks of the season. I was very close to signing to play for Queensland in the Sheffield Shield later in the year, but after tossing it over in my mind I finally pulled out. I was very interested in playing in Australia; by common consent it is the toughest form of first-class cricket in the world outside Test matches, and the four-day game suited me. The money was good and the whole package seemed attractive. Yet I sensed that all wasn't quite right about the deal. The main sponsors of Queensland jumped the gun a little by saying that I'd signed for them when there were still a few things that needed to be ironed out. It even appeared on Teletext back in Britain that I was going to play for them, even though I hadn't formally agreed to anything. An executive of New South Wales came in with a counter-offer, but I soon got wind that their players didn't want me. I knew that a lot of Australian cricketers don't particularly like overseas players coming into their State cricket, getting a lot more money than them, so I knew that the New South Wales deal was likely to collapse.

Yet somehow I felt I wouldn't be totally welcome at Queensland either – even though when Worcestershire had a short tour out there in April, there had seemed plenty of warmth from their players. I'm the kind of person who has to feel right in a dressing room; I hate cliques and back-stabbing and I didn't want to feel at all unwelcome. I mulled it over for several weeks when I got back to England, talked it over with my parents and then with Basil D'Oliveira. Initially Basil said I must go; like me, he knew that the experience of playing that class of cricket would be very valuable. Yet he sensed I wasn't a hundred per cent in favour. There were distractions; I thought I could do with a winter away from first-class cricket to recharge my batteries. If all went according to plan and I was a success at Test level, I might be on tour with England for a lot of years to come in the near future. I also fancied a holiday visiting my family for a few weeks back in Zimbabwe, especially when I learned that my sister was pregnant with her first child. The idea of relaxing in Zimbabwe with all of them definitely appealed, even though I knew that that wouldn't be a practical boost to my career.

Basil said eventually, 'Well, go back to Zimbabwe then,' and I felt a lot better for talking to him. My mind was made up. I turned down Queensland. Some people out there slagged me off, saying that I had been trying to winkle a better deal out of them, but that is simply not true. I just didn't feel right about going there at that stage of my life – a year later, when the offer came through again, I was delighted to commit myself to them for their 1990/1 season.

I admit that I let the whole thing prey on my mind for far too long. It dragged on for about a month as I tossed the options around and it definitely affected my form at the start of the 1989 season with Worcestershire. I ought to have made a quick decision and followed my instinct but I worried too much about it. The unreliable wickets at New Road also contributed to my negative state of mind. I was just like the other Worcestershire boys – lacking confidence at the crease, stuck in the 'halfway house' position, not knowing how to do something that we all know instinctively from the time we were kids. Usually I don't complain about such things in the dressing room – I just go out there and play and don't moan when I'm out – but it was hard to remain philosophical when you're worried about getting smacked on the face or fingers by bowlers who aren't really all that good. It was all right in the nets, but somehow I couldn't take the confidence I built up there into the middle with me.

Earlier in the year I had thought about the possibility of getting a thousand runs in May again for the second year in a row. I knew that had never been done, so I thought, 'Why not?' I started off well enough with 173 not out for Worcestershire against the MCC at Lord's, but I didn't get another first-class hundred for two months, taking me sixteen innings in all. That is definitely not my style and I kept brooding about it. How much could I blame the New Road wickets? How much is down to the individual batsman? What is wrong with my footwork? It was too easy to blame it on the

Reader ball, with its larger seams; I hadn't had too much difficulty with it the previous summer. Relations between the players and our groundsman, Roy McLaren, were getting strained purely because we were looking for scapegoats. It wasn't Roy's fault – there had been a problem for a couple of seasons at New Road and he was doing his best to rid the pitches of uneven bounce, but it was not going to happen overnight for him. When we lost five games in a row and tumbled out of the Benson and Hedges Cup after losing to the Combined Universities, it looked as if we were in for a nightmare season. It was significant that I scored a hundred in that match and never looked as if I was in any sort of form. I just opted for crease occupation and tried to churn out the runs.

I was pretty difficult to live with during the month of May. I'd come home, tell Jackie it was all the fault of the wickets and sit in front of the TV, brooding. Usually I can't wait to get out into the middle when it's my turn to bat, but now I was dragging myself off my chair. As usual when I'm worried about something I sought out Basil D'Oliveira. He didn't mince his words and told me to snap out of it and to remember it was a long season. 'Here you are, moping around, and it's only the middle of May,' he said. 'You've got another four months to go. Forget what's happened and look to the future. Don't change your natural way of batting.' I felt better for getting things off my chest after talking to someone I respect so much. Basil knew what we were all going through, but he wouldn't allow us any self-pity. I had to smile whenever one of our supporters sidled up and said, 'Not the usual Graeme Hick today, was it?' and just content myself with something along the lines of 'Just shows I'm human, doesn't it?' I was hurting inside, but there was no point in taking it out on well-meaning supporters.

It started to come back slowly once my parents arrived on their annual holiday. It's funny how things seem to happen when they fly in! When we were playing Derbyshire at New Road, Mum noticed that I was crouching too much at the crease. She had just arrived, but it was the first thing she noticed. That underlined my anxiety, but it helped force me to stand up straighter and assert myself. A few days later we went up to Harrogate to play in the Tilcon Trophy and I got a few runs, this time in my usual style. I even started to hit the ball over the top again, something I had hardly tried so far in the season. In our next championship match – at Sheffield against Yorkshire – I got that elusive hundred and things clicked into place. And yes – Mum and Dad were there to see it. I was glad that I had spent such a long time out in the middle a week earlier in a benefit match for Paul Pridgeon, getting the feel of bat on ball and recapturing the rhythm of batting. I had got 0 the day before in another benefit match and the lads pulled my leg when I scampered a quick single to get off the mark. I decided to bat out our innings and even though one or two of the boys suggested similarities with Geoffrey Boycott, they knew what I was trying to do. You need to feel instinctively comfortable at the crease, not expecting a delivery to knock you over for no apparent reason.

Our roll towards the championship really started in the early days of July when we beat Northants by an innings and then beat Lancashire, two dangerous sides. When I went out to bat at Northampton, it all suddenly fell into place. Off my first ball, I guided Curtley Ambrose to the cover-point boundary and thought, 'That's not a bad piece of timing.' In the next over, I pushed forward to a ball and saw it skim to the extra-cover boundary. Guaranteed to make you feel a batsman! I made 111 that day and for the rest of the season I was much happier with my form. I made almost a thousand runs in August and the worries of April and May seemed dim and distant, as Basil had forecast. Not until late July did I feel happy about batting at New Road, when Roy McLaren consulted the Test and County Cricket Board's Pitches Inspector, Harry Brind, before preparing two pitches for the games against Surrey and Kent. I made 85 and 147 in those games and, although they played low and slow, at least the bounce was uniform. By the time we played Lancashire in the Nat-West Trophy quarter-finals at home, I felt the season was only just starting for me. Again I just pushed one for four to get off the mark and felt very encouraged at my timing. I made 90 not out, won the game with a six and at last I felt I had the taste back.

Shortly after that Lancashire match, I played one of the most satisfying innings of my career. We just had to beat Somerset to stay in the championship race and they set us 300 in fifty-seven overs. It was a stiff declaration by Vic Marks but we couldn't complain because he and the Somerset bowlers had suffered a fair amount at our hands in recent years. Again Tim Curtis was an ideal partner for me in another big stand. He did the counting and I just played! At one time we were up to around nine an over, but we got away with a few shots, kept the pressure up and I managed to time sweetly a few that went for six. We paced it just right and I was absolutely delighted with my 136 not out, as we won by five wickets.

I shall never forget the overwhelming feeling of satisfaction as I walked towards the pavilion steps with everyone wildly excited after we had won. So many people were patting me on the back and it was great to see all my team-mates waiting at the top of the stairs to congratulate me. I can still see Richard Illingworth coming forward to be the first to say, 'Well done', and soon I was mobbed by the boys. I had done my job properly and the extra satisfaction was that it had won us the game and set up the push towards the title, when everybody had written us off a month earlier. I don't get my enjoyment purely from scoring a hundred; I get it from batting well for a certain length of time against good bowling in a run-chase when the bowlers and I are all trying to come out on top. If you can manipulate it your way in such a tense situation – looking up at the scoreboard, picking up the singles, doing your sums, cashing in on loose deliveries – then it's a marvellous feeling when you win. That was just about the best chasing innings I have played so far and the context was so important. I batted for the respect of my team-mates as well as for the result that day, and it was a memorable experience.

We were destined to win the 1989 championship, I think. When we needed to, we kept squeezing out the results. We were getting occasional wickets with bad balls, taking marvellous catches and getting home in a run-chase. Everyone deals in 'ifs' and 'buts' towards the end of a season, but we just kept our eye on the main chance and didn't dwell on maybes. Our championship win that year wasn't as popular as in 1988, because we were no longer an unfashionable side. We were now the glamour boys, expected to pick up the prizes.

I think the neutrals were probably pleased that we lost the Nat-West Trophy semi-final to Warwickshire, because they weren't as fancied as us and were due a final at Lord's. Not that we didn't try our utmost that day at Edgbaston. I am still trying to work out how I managed to nick one from Dermot Reeve to the wicket-keeper soon after I came in. I watched my dismissal that night over and over again on video and I seemed to get everything right – but my bat came down crooked and I nicked it.

So Warwickshire's success at Lord's was popular and I think many cricket lovers felt sorry for Essex that they didn't win the championship. They lost 25 points for preparing a substandard pitch at Southend and that enabled us to leapfrog above them and hang on to our narrow lead right to the end. The Essex administrators showed what they thought of the TCCB's decision by paying their players the bonus they would have got had they won the title, but I had no sympathy for them. The rules were laid down at the start of the season and everyone knew the score. They got away with it in the first match at Southend when the Kent game was over inside two days, and the next one against Yorkshire was also a nightmare for batting.

Of course, they pointed to our New Road pitches and asked why we got away without punishment, but they forget that our club took steps to try to improve the situation. After the game against the Australians ended inside two days at the start of May (on a pitch which both teams considered to look like a beautiful batting wicket), our club called in Harry Brind to advise Roy McLaren in his pitch preparation. Both groundsmen tried very hard to get a fairer contest between bat and ball, and towards the end of the season the bounce was at least regular, even if the wickets were playing slow and low. So at least Worcestershire took steps to avoid what turned out to be an historic penalty. After all, the TCCB had appointed a Pitches Consultant, so it made sense to seek his advice from early in May. Anyway, we had much the best of our game against Essex in Colchester in August; if we hadn't dropped a couple of catches we would have beaten them easily and made this kind of discussion pretty irrelevant. And we could always argue that rain denied us the chance to gain maximum points in our last game against Glamorgan at Pontypridd which would have taken us well ahead of Essex, penalty or no penalty.

Enough of this – mustn't get involved with 'ifs' and 'buts'. It's typical of the Essex players that they were still moaning about losing the 1989 championship the following summer. They do like things their own way on the field – they moan loudly when decisions by the umpires go against them. Perhaps they have become too used to success in the last decade. I wonder what their excuse is for losing out on the 1990 championship? It can't be a deduction of 25 points this time.

It was a pity that our two championship victories came with a bit of a cloud attached – just one point ahead of Kent in 1988, then the moans from Essex in 1989. I feel we weren't given as much credit as we deserved for coming with a late rush in 1989. The injuries would have finished off a squad with an inferior team spirit, and in Steve McEwan and Stu Lampitt we found the bowlers to win us matches. The variable quality of some of the New Road pitches definitely affected us more than the opposition because they didn't have to play on it more than once a season. You don't normally have to think about the basics of batting other than the actual execution of the stroke once you get to first-class standard, but all of us in the home dressing room questioned our techniques at some stage or other that summer. Our detractors might like to note that, far from being favoured by home advantage, seven of our twelve championship victories came away from New Road. From the end of July, we won six of our last eight championship games – the others were a washout at Pontypridd and the best of a drawn match at Colchester. That's the form of champions. Professionalism, good captaincy from Phil Neale and fine bowling made it happen for us, just as we were being dismissed as no-hopers. Very satisfying.

So the 1989 season proved to be a vital one for me. I am sure that it hardened me up. A spell of failure is necessary to make a cricketer reassess where he's going, to force him to take a long, hard look at himself. I was getting runs in the one-day games early in the season, but nothing in the championship, yet instead of looking at that positively I was prone to self-pity. Negative vibes in a dressing room can be very contagious and, try as I might, I couldn't stop myself from being sucked into the sense of defeatism. A batsman sitting with his pads on, waiting to go in next, shouldn't be subjected to tirades about the poor pitch from someone who's now out – and at times we were all guilty of that. As Basil told me, you have to play the ball, rather than the reputation of pitch or bowler. It's too early to be in despair when there are almost four months of a season still to play. Admittedly my mood wasn't exactly settled at the start of the season, due to my preoccupation with the Queensland offer – but that was mainly my fault. Perhaps I was too over-sensitive about what the Aussies might make of me, perhaps I was too aware that they don't rate anyone who hasn't got runs in Australia. I wouldn't make the same mistake again. The Graeme Hick that went out to Queensland late in 1990 was a tougher cricketer for the experiences of 1989.

CHAPTER THIRTEEN

Biding My Time

THE figures may suggest otherwise, but I don't feel I was at my best in the summer of 1990, my last season before I became eligible for England. At this stage of my career, I found myself thinking that I needed an extra challenge. That has usually come along just at the right time for me, and there were times last season when I found myself feeling a little jaded and stale. I still tried my hardest for Worcestershire every time I went on the pitch – I don't know any other way – but I didn't feel as comfortable at the crease as I usually do. The wickets at New Road were more consistent but very slow and I had trouble with my timing for long periods. The ball just didn't come on to the bat as I would have liked, and the home games – and some away as well – were often fairly boring. It was a batsman's summer due to the fine weather, the reduced number of strands on the ball's seam, and the improved wickets, but that doesn't always lead to the best type of cricket. When the ball's not coming on to the bat, that means you take an extra hour to get a certain score, the opposition have the same problem and the game drifts along until the final afternoon of a three-day match when a declaration leads to a frantic run-chase.

I may be a little over-critical of myself here, but even though I ended up with a first-class average of more than 90 and scored 2300 runs, I was disappointed that I didn't score more hundreds. A total of fourteen half-centuries and eight hundreds isn't the return I would have liked. I passed 75 four times without getting a hundred and that wasn't satisfactory. I can accept it when I get out in a run-chase but not when I'm in no real hurry. When well-meaning supporters say 'Well played', it kills the value of being praised for something that isn't all that special. I haven't found it a burden to myself that I have scored so many runs when still so young, but I know that too much is expected of me from certain quarters. Not my team-mates, I hasten to add, because they know that cricket is a difficult game, not an exact science. I felt last season that many of our supporters and the media were waiting for me to fail because it's different and therefore something to talk about. Sometimes I felt slightly envious of young players who came in and played some lovely, carefree shots against us. I would stand beside Damian D'Oliveira in the slips and say, 'You know, Dolly, I used to play like that,' and Dolly would smile, knowing what I meant.

I know that if I had got out playing my shots a few years ago, no one would have minded – but now if I lose my wicket through carelessness, many will say, 'What's he got out for?' If I was given the freedom to go out and just enjoy myself, maybe it would be great for me, but I know that I have to be *got* out now, otherwise it might be suggested that I don't care so much about my batting any more. Of course I do – it's just different for me now. The bowlers and opposition captains don't give me any favours any more and I have to work for my runs, because they have established where I like to play my strokes. No complaints about that – we live in a hard profession. Now I find one of the difficult parts of batting is to keep my concentration at its sharpest. Several times last season, I found myself thinking. 'This is a flat wicket. If I stay in here for three hours, I've got another hundred.' That is an aim in itself and I still love churning out the hundreds, but the fact that batting was often easier than in previous seasons at New Road took away a little bit of personal satisfaction. I don't consider it a burden at all to have high standards. I think that should apply to all professionally minded people in various walks of life. If you don't have high standards, you just drift away to be a nobody. Perhaps I am thinking too deeply about my batting, but better that than being complacent, thinking I've got it made. Deep down, I know that I got away with it a little bit in 1990, despite all those runs. At times they came rather cheaply and I wasn't fooled.

I rarely felt totally happy with my hands on the bat last

season. I like just to pick up my bat and feel my hands are an extension of the blade. It all has to feel just right, yet several times Phil Neale noticed that I was fretting and fidgeting with my gloves while at the crease. Golfers don't like to have a crease across the palm of their hand and batsmen don't feel comfortable if they have to keep pulling the inners and their batting gloves into position. I went through a lot of batting gloves last season, and for a time I used inners that were thinner than usual – but it never felt a hundred per cent. Phil Neale told me to relax and just go out and play but it became a psychological thing and I never really settled in my stance.

I felt fine at the start of the season, coming back very fit from Zimbabwe after a refreshing and enjoyable break visiting my family. Early on I played well to get 97 against Nottinghamshire on a New Road pitch that had a bit of pace and encouraged the seamers. I was bowled on the back foot by Franklyn Stephenson when it hardly bounced and, although I was looking for a really big score, I couldn't do anything about my dismissal, because I wasn't technically at fault. I wanted a good season to press my claims for England consideration the next year, but then I lost five weeks after picking up my first serious injury.

When we played the New Zealanders, a ball from Danny Morrison came through a little quicker than I expected and I was late on to it. It hit me on the left index finger and I knew it was a bad one. I've had sore knuckles from blows in recent seasons but I've managed to bat on – this time I knew the difference. I thought, 'There's a long season ahead,' and came off for treatment. The finger was broken, so I had to sit it out for a month. I kept myself fit, but moped around a little towards the end of that month because I couldn't play golf for a time. But I knew it was important to let the break heal. When I came back, it was amazing how much weaker my left hand had become; after batting for half an hour, it felt tired, so I had to work on building it back up to full strength.

I suppose my best innings was the 252 not out against Glamorgan at Abergavenny. I wanted to get back to scoring double hundreds again, having missed out on one in 1989, and it was nice to get on a flat wicket with the ball coming on to the bat for once. It wasn't a real tester, because the boundaries were fairly short and the bowling wasn't all that penetrative, but it was good to build an innings and feel I was playing somewhere near the standards I set myself. After that innings, there was a lot of media talk about me setting up a new world record for the greatest number of runs scored without being dismissed. I wasn't too fussed about that – it's not much of an achievement in my eyes – and I was amused that when I was out in the next game at Derby for 53, it was said that I had failed! Talking of records, I was much happier to become the youngest ever to reach fifty first-class hundreds. I understand I have about another five years on my side to be the youngest to get a hundred centuries and that is one record I would be happy to set. A fair number of batsmen have got fifty hundreds, but not many reach the century mark. I'll keep an eye on that one as the years go by . . .

I was amazed that my feat of a thousand runs by the end of May wasn't matched last season. The wickets were perfect for large scores, the weather was ideal and the bowlers were more ineffective than they had been in 1988. In a sense I was glad that no one did it. I like being part of a select group who have got there and if the batting conditions stay like those of last year there could be a whole batch of players who emulate me and Glenn Turner. In many ways it felt strange to be overshadowed by other batsmen in 1990, but I wasn't bothered by that. People like Gooch, Fairbrother, Cook, Tendulkar and Atherton grabbed a lot of headlines and good luck to them. I was quite happy being in the background, because I know that when I am eligible for England, there will be a lot of hype flying around, even if I don't get picked.

I also know there'll be a lot of talk about whether I have the big-match temperament. My failure in the 1990 Benson and Hedges Cup Final will be used as evidence that I might lack the necessary on the big occasion. That has been set alongside my other Lord's failure, in the Nat-West Final in 1989. Well, if they want to knock, let them; everyone is entitled to an opinion, but I worry about it a good deal less than anyone else. I'm not being blasé about it, but on each occasion I was turned over by a very good bowler – Angus Fraser in 1988 and Wasim Akram last season. Wasim has a very fast arm action and he has that ability to swing the ball either way at speed. It is difficult batting against a left-armer who puts the ball across you and also brings it back in. You have to play your shot as late as you can, but the fact that he delivers the ball a yard quicker than you think is a big plus in his favour.

So you need to get in and face him for a few overs, just to work out what he's doing, but I only had three balls from him at Lord's and he got me with a good one that I nicked to the wicket-keeper. I would have been a good deal more worried if I'd got out to a long-hop from a medium-pace trundler, but when he did me again the next day in the Refuge League, there was talk that I was Wasim Akram's rabbit. Well, I thought I played quite well against him on the Sunday, because he swung it both ways from around and then over the wicket and he only got me out when I chopped on towards the end of the innings as we needed quick runs. After both games, Basil D'Oliveira told me that he didn't think I would do well at Lord's. He noticed that I was fidgeting a lot before I went in to bat – something I don't normally do – and I must admit I felt a little tense. It wasn't the big occasion – I love the idea of batting in front of a full house at Lord's – but I was still bothered about my hands on the bat and I would have liked to have had more match practice in the run-in to the final. Because of a quirk in the fixture list, we had a lot of gaps in June and July and we never really got going. After my lay-off through injury, I needed time out in the middle. On the day, a world-class bowler got the better of me. That's cricket.

I was more concerned about losing our Nat-West Cup quarter-final than missing out at Lord's. Seven times out of ten we would have beaten Northants and I still can't believe that Ian Botham was left high and dry at the end, with us losing by four runs. It seemed as if Ian had won us the game once he had sorted out his timing and started hitting clean sixes. All we needed was for the later batsmen to support him, to give him the strike and to keep our heads. But we blew it. We bowled badly at the start of their innings, when we should have kept it tight and allowed that to prey on their nerves. Instead we fed them with a diet of half-volleys and long-hops and they got away. The atmosphere in our dressing room was worse that day than when we lost so easily to Lancashire in the Benson's Final. When you can see defeat coming a long way off, you can adjust to it before the actual moment when it's over and you then have to face the public. Yet in tense games like that Northants one, we were on a high and then, a few balls later, we were totally deflated. That was a game that we lost, rather than Northants winning it through their efforts.

So by the start of August we were out of everything and we had to knuckle down and look for a decent finish to the championship season. Considering that we were second bottom in the table by the end of July, I think we did very well to finish fourth, with Hampshire easing us out of third position on the very last day. We won five of our last twelve games and, if we had just been a little more penetrative with our bowling, we would have pushed Middlesex hard. After all, we only lost one game in the entire championship season, just like Middlesex, but in three matches (against Kent, Derbyshire and Hampshire), the full points were there for the taking, but we just couldn't bowl out their tail. We badly missed Graham Dilley, because he has shown since 1987 that he can knock over a tail with his extra pace. But his right knee continued to trouble him and he could only play in a few games; when he did, he showed his true value to us. He remains a high-class strike bowler, capable of getting out the best batsmen. We can't complain about our bad luck with injuries, though – it's the same for all sides. In 1988 and 1989, we had a lot of injuries to our bowlers, but somebody would come along and roll the batters over. This time it didn't happen, but we have nobody to blame but ourselves.

At Worcester we are all well aware that to win championship matches we have to look to bowl the opposition out twice. In the past two seasons, we have won nineteen championship matches and, apart from one game, that has been through taking twenty wickets each time. The exception was the match against Somerset at New

Road in August 1989 when I helped us to win that thrilling run-chase. In other words, we know that opposition captains are wary about setting us targets. It will be no easier in 1991, now that we have signed Tom Moody to replace me as the overseas player. In his one season with Warwickshire, Tom showed what a fine attacking batsman he is and he won a few matches after a declaration left Warwickshire needing to go for the runs against the clock. There are going to be times next season when we will be asked to chase ridiculous totals, but I can't see how much higher the captains can go without making a farce of a three-day game. In the last couple of seasons, we have regularly been asked to get around six an over stretching over a long period – say fifty-plus overs. I can't see how they can expect us to go for about eight an over because unless two batsmen get in and really whack it around for a long time, such a target is unrealistic. We won't get many favours, but then I don't believe that's been the case for us since we got home in a few run-chases between 1986 and 1988. The old formula of bowling out sides twice remains our best bet for the future, so I hope our bowlers can regain their sharpness and that the wickets give a better balance between bat and ball.

CHAPTER FOURTEEN

Thoughts on Batting

MANY people are kind enough to say that I make batting look easy. Well, to me some parts of it are, but there are other, elusive areas that need constant attention. Sometimes when I'm out there at the crease I wonder what the crowd are thinking. I'll suddenly say to myself, 'Do they think I'm playing as well as ever? Do they think I'm struggling? I suppose they assume another hundred's inevitable.' I now know that I can't always turn in the performances that are expected of me – it's just not possible. I am now more aware of external pressure – coming from those who want me to succeed and those who know it's a good story if I keep failing. I don't let that bother me any more, after my experiences of 1989 when runs were so scarce in first-class cricket for so long.

That summer was good for my mental development. I had known that the first full season after breaking on to the county scene was going to be a big test for me and when I got 2000 runs that year, I was delighted. Nowadays people expect me to do well every day, but I won't let that get to me. I now try to approach my batting in a relaxed yet serious way because I believe that if you're happy with life, you're halfway there, as long as you have the natural ability. You need to be relaxed to time the ball properly – that is one of the fundamentals of batting. That came to me a few years ago when I wasn't getting many runs in Zimbabwe club cricket. I went for a game of golf with some friends and suddenly I started to time the ball sweetly. My godfather said, 'You'll get a hundred tomorrow,' and he was right. My co-ordination suddenly linked with my timing and I was making contact with the ball at the right moment. It can go and return just like that.

At first-class level, batting must be an instinctive thing. You have a system in your mind that you must play to, and when the ball is bowled the system takes over automatically. There just isn't the time to think about how you should play the stroke. You don't think, 'Short ball – play back.' Your eyes see the ball and your body takes over spontaneously. My initial movements are totally natural and I won't ever change that. Much is made of my being a front-foot player, but I don't think I'm all that different from many batters, who have an initial forward movement, then rock back. As a tall man with a long reach it makes sense for me to launch into the drive when I can, but I don't feel I neglect my back-foot play. I just don't think about what shots to play – I'm not programmed.

I'm sure that if I got into the England side and failed, I would start to wonder if my technique was right for the amount of short-pitched bowling you get from the West Indies. I would probably go and see Basil D'Oliveira and ask him if I should learn to play more off the back foot. I know what he would say – 'You've scored enough runs playing your own way, so don't change it now. Go out and play naturally.' So many of the Australian batsmen on the 1989 tour impressed the pundits because of their textbook style, with the bat still on the ground as the bowler ran in. Fair enough – they were successful – but that method also suited them, it was natural to them. The same applies if you prefer to have your bat in the air. My stance hasn't really changed since I was seventeen when Bill Bourne slipped a few fast yorkers through me in the school nets and made it clear that I'd struggle in adult cricket unless I sorted out my backlift. It felt comfortable to have my bat raised to the level of the stumps and I've stuck with it ever since. It's not baseball style like Graham Gooch. I think I'm more nine o'clock on the dial, compared to Gooch's eleven o'clock but the crucial thing is that it suits both of us.

If you're as tall as me, you tend to prefer to play upright; shorter batsmen tend to crouch and that obviously suits them. The important element is keeping your eye on the ball as it is being delivered. I believe that the head should be over the line of the stumps, with the right eye over middle and off stumps for the right-hand batsman. That way, I know that anything in that channel will hit the stumps and that a ball outside that area will be missing. If I took guard and crouched lower, then my head would be outside the line of the stumps, so such a stance would contravene one of the basics of batting – knowing exactly where your stumps are. Ever since my schooldays, I have taken middle-and-leg guard because I was told that my height meant I needed to come across my stumps. If I took centre I would be in danger of lunging too far across, so two legs it was and it's stayed with me.

When I'm waiting to go into bat, I try not to theorise too much. By now I will know what the particular bowlers are capable of, having played a few years in England, so I bear that in mind. I'll see how the wicket is playing for a couple of overs, but after that I'm happy to be distracted and have a laugh with my team-mates. I'll tell myself not to get too tense. When I go in, I'll be cautious early on, looking to bat for a long time, but if I get three half-volleys, I hope that will get me pretty quickly to 12. It's funny how a nought preys on every batsman's mind. There is no difference really between 0 and 1, yet we all want to get away from 0, don't we? If I play in a benefit match and I get three or four, nobody remembers that, but if I get a duck, that keeps the crowd and the players going for a day or two. I guarantee that somewhere the bowler will catch up with you and remind you he got you out for a duck. Even in games like that, I want to get off the mark. I still haven't got a 'pair' in first-class cricket (although I've gone close with 0 and 1) and that is something I would gladly avoid throughout my career.

Some batsmen like to approach their innings in stages, getting to ten, then twenty, establishing command along the way. In my case, I just like to stay in there as long as I can, telling myself that if I am in for about three hours, I will have a hundred, by my usual rate of scoring. I get annoyed with myself if I don't punish the bad ball; I work on the assumption that I will get a lot of very good deliveries in a season, some of which will dismiss me, so I want to get boundaries off the bad ones. When I bat, I have a small visual plan of where the fielders are positioned – it's a sense of their exact location when I'm waiting for the ball to be delivered. When I'm playing well, I don't hit the fielders – I seem to be able to bisect the field. It's not something that I work at: I seem to be able to anticipate where to position the ball. I will have taken note of the field placing when waiting to go out to bat, and I will hopefully be aware of the particularly good fielders, but it would be wrong to place too much emphasis on those fields before I get out there.

In the last couple of years, I have noticed specific fields for me. Mid-on, midwicket and mid-off tend to be pushed a lot straighter and deeper for me, because they know I like to drive straight ('through the V' as the coaches call it). That tends to cut off a productive area for me, but I won't panic. In a three-day game, I'm quite happy to push to deep mid-on or mid-off and refuse a possible single. I'll try to get my timing right for those shots, knowing that if I'm still there in a couple of hours, I can beef up the power. Some counties have tried two gullys for me; I can see why because I like to run the ball down to third man and also like to stand up and go for the crashing square cut. Certainly if I'm looking for the shot off the back foot, I might play it uppishly if there is sudden, extra bounce. That tends to happen with the slightly slower bowler when I'm feeling more confident to stand up and hit him. If he suddenly gets extra bounce from nowhere and I'm committed to the square cut, that can result in an edge. With the quicker bowlers who are getting bounce regularly, I tend not to play a shot, so the two gullys are then wasted. I can think of better places to position a fielder for me, but I don't think it would be a very good idea to reveal more!

I suppose any batsman of class prefers to be dismissed by a catch, rather than any other way. Certainly I like to get part of my bat on the ball if I am bowled – an inside edge or dragging it on when I get too near the ball for the cut, or the ball has come back sharply off the seam. You tend to worry if you miss the ball by a long way and it hits the stumps. That means a misjudgement and perhaps faulty footwork. I'm not often out lbw because I do tend to get forward enough with my long reach. Many batsmen are inclined to delude themselves over lbws, but I don't see the point. On average I would say that I get a marginal one a couple of times a season, and I can't complain about that. Sometimes I'm hit on the pads and I think, 'That's got to be close,' and I get away with it. Five overs later, I may be given out lbw when it wasn't so close. That's just one of those things – there will always be human error in cricket. As for run-outs – I don't believe in them. I've never been a great one for suicidal singles. I think there are more than enough ways to get yourself out without something like that. If there's any doubt at all, I'll shout 'No!' There's always the next ball to make up for that missed single. So I suppose a thin edge to the keeper or to first slip is the preferred method of dismissal for any batsman who tries to play properly; that means you have slightly misjudged the situation or got a terrific delivery you were good enough to touch.

Some batsmen tend to freeze up when they get into the 90s, but I don't see the need for that. You've obviously been out in the middle for a fair time to get that amount of runs, and even if you have scratched around, you're bound to have played some good shots. So I just play it on its merits, telling myself that a half-volley when I'm in the 90s ought to be despatched, while a good ball must be respected even though I feel I'm going well. I don't get out a lot in the 90s and I hope that's because I don't panic. The more often you get into that stage, the easier it is to get through. I have got to my hundred in singles, sometimes with two sixes, or three fours – it varies so much, but the vital ingredient is to stay calm and bide your time. I tell myself that if I can see it through for another half-hour, then I will have my hundred. Anyway, 99 is far better than 0! I've often wondered why a hundred seems to be the preferred magic figure – why not a hundred and fifty? Perhaps it's because you are going from two to three figures. Whatever the reason, I like getting centuries and if I have gone a few games without getting one I start to wonder what's wrong. A batsman needs that kind of hunger.

I do enjoy hitting sixes – it's the macho 'Take that!' shot for a bowler, some of whom can be demoralised by the shot. Yet a four off certain bowlers can be just as satisfying. When you lean forward early on in your innings and see the ball skim through the covers even though you feel you've just blocked it – that is a great feeling – it tells you the timing is in good order today. That must be a killer for some bowlers. Yet no bowler really likes being hit for six (as I know from personal experience). There's only two runs in the difference, but there is a psychological gulf between a four and a six. Some sixes just die over the boundary rope, especially off a slow bowler and at other times it's particularly enjoyable to ping a ball over the ropes that felt as if it was only going for a four. Catching it just right in the meat of the bat is a lovely feeling. Normally my sixes are pretty flat, but I remember one during last season at New Road when I hit Phil Bainbridge over long-on into the trees at the Digliss End. That went a long way. So did some of those I hit at Neath in 1986, when we had a successful run-chase. I remember one off Nick Cook when the English Counties side came to Zimbabwe. I opened up my stance, hit it against the spin and it soared over midwicket like a seven iron. That was a blow rather than a stroke and another one like that came during my innings against Somerset at New Road in 1989 when we chased 300 to win a vital game. Adrian Jones bowled me one that didn't feel right when it left the bat, but then it soared over the longest part of the boundary, at midwicket. I couldn't believe it had gone so far – it was mishit.

I try very hard not to slog sixes. I want to get them properly, but some purists are offended that I loft the ball. One chap walked past me last season and said, 'You'll never be a great player. You hit the ball too much in the air.' I just laughed, as I thought about all the great players who hit a lot of sixes. If you hit the ball far enough and you know what you're doing, what is wrong with a six? If you keep getting stumped or you miscue it, that is different, but the textbooks encourage a confident batsman to go down the wicket and get to the pitch of the ball. The lofted drive is an accepted, orthodox stroke and I can't think of any modern cricket followers who don't like seeing that shot when it is properly executed.

It does help if you use a proper bat, one that is nicely balanced with a lot of meat in the drive area. Duncan Fearnley, our chairman, has done me proud over the years with the bats he makes for me. I went on his books in 1984 when I was playing for Kidderminster in the Birmingham League and for Worcestershire seconds. I had just made the record score for Kidderminster (182 not out), using a Gunn and Moore bat, and Duncan said, 'If you'd used a decent bat, you'd have got two hundred.' Shortly after that, my bat broke, so I went to Duncan and asked for 'a decent bat'. It's gone on from there and Duncan keeps coming up with beauties. They've been as heavy as three pounds in the past but they are lighter now. Pick-up is very important to me and I like a lot of wood high up on the blade. I prefer a short handle, so that I can feel the weight of the bat close to my hands, instead of further down the blade.

I can remember most of my innings in first-class cricket and how I got out, but I don't find that at all surprising. It's my job and I ought to be able to learn from mistakes that cost me my wicket. If you're a second-hand car salesman, you would know the price of cars a few years back, so what's the difference? I can recall being caught and bowled by Tim Munton after I had made 126 in the Bank Holiday local derby at Edgbaston in 1987. It was a good, waist-high catch but the reason I remember the dismissal was because I pushed forward too early, trying to drive on the up. I didn't quite get there and caught it higher on the bat than I intended. That dismissal highlighted one of the problems of playing straight; if I had been looking to work the ball either side of the bowler, I might have got away with that piece of mistiming. So after that I worked hard at still playing straight, but watching the ball on to the bat, making sure I didn't mistime anything early in my innings. Common sense really, if you take your job seriously. A batsman also has to try to work out what's in the bowler's mind. You tend to expect the yorker after the short-pitched delivery, and that often goes for four because there is no surprise element and you don't have to move your feet for the yorker. An intelligent bowler will double-bluff you with a good-length one after the 'throat ball', so you have to move your feet and get into position. That often gets a wicket because it's not obvious.

A lot of umpires and bowlers will say that nobody 'walks' any more in county cricket. I don't agree with that. Certainly I don't hang around, making the umpire's job difficult if I know that I've touched it. There are perhaps a couple of situations in my county career when I've been given out badly in the first innings, then got off the hook in the second innings because no one appealed. If there had been an appeal I would have walked straight off, but, without one, I saw no reason to sacrifice my wicket. Apart from that I have always gone when I was certain I had nicked it – that is the key to it, because there are times when the batsman is genuinely not sure and then he is entitled to stay where he is. Damian D'Oliveira always walks when he knows he has hit it, but I have been at the other end when I am certain he has got a nick and he has waited for the decision. He just wasn't sure and so he was justified in letting the umpire decide. There are still a lot of batsmen like Dolly and me around. We know there are going to be some bad decisions over a season, but if you try to manipulate the system to suit yourself, you can't complain when it goes against you. You can't be a selective walker. When the West Indies made such a fuss about the alleged nick to the keeper off Ian Bishop in May 1988, they didn't know that if I had been sure I had touched it I would have gone, despite the frustration of just missing out on a personal landmark.

I am aware that my career has given a lot of work to statisticians and kept them happy over the past few years, but I don't bat for that kind of glory. I don't play the game for myself, I play it for my team and in the process I also get personal pleasure if things are going well. I'm lucky to be able to bat at number three, so I have time to build an innings; when you're at number five or six, you're sometimes short of the space to get yourself established and then you start worrying about your average, but I don't have to at three. I love the pressure involved in trying to win a game against the clock – that's why the Somerset game in 1989 was so satisfactory. It is getting more difficult now for Worcestershire to win games in a run-chase. I know there is a responsibility on me in these situations and I like that, but the opposition tend to close up the field against me now. In my early days in championship cricket, I was new to the bowlers, and they used to feed my strengths, giving me width so that I could cut, and pitching it up, inviting the drive. Now more and more are bowling straight at me, with mid-off and mid-on deep. They're hoping that I'll get myself out through frustration, but it's all part of the learning game. I shall just have to keep occupying the crease, hoping to wear them down.

When you're new to the county game, you just go out there and hit the ball, but the longer you play it, the more complicated it becomes. So much more is expected of you – you get a nought and people ask what's gone wrong. I've paid the price since 1988, when I scored all those runs, especially the 405 not out. I have set myself very high standards, but I tell myself that I am capable of getting another 400 at some time. If I didn't think that, it would be almost like admitting I have declined since 1988, which I don't think is the case. I aim for 2000 first-class runs every season, a figure that is perfectly possible if you're free from injuries and play around thirty-five innings a summer.

I also see no reason why I can't keep clocking up the hundreds as my career continues. If I play well enough to get into the England team, that will mean I am scoring runs – and hundreds. If I manage to establish myself as a Test batsman – and I know that is a big 'if' – there will be plenty of chances to get in on flat wickets. Not every Test match involves ducking and diving against four fast West Indian bowlers. There are other Test attacks that aren't quite so relentless. Any batsman must fancy playing five-day cricket on a flat pitch, despite all the other pressures involved in Test cricket. It seems to me that one of the big differences is that your usual rate of scoring dips – in the county game, a confident batsman with a good range of strokes should get around 75 a session, whereas in Tests you would do well to make 50 in the two hours between intervals. Of course there are other complications to playing at the highest level and I just hope I get the chance to experience them. Whatever happens, I owe it to myself and to Worcestershire to maintain my county form.

CHAPTER FIFTEEN

Zimbabwe's Test Prospects

MY own career underlines the difficulty Zimbabwe faces when there's talk about becoming another of the Test nations. Given different circumstances there's part of me which would love still to be involved with Zimbabwe's cricket, but early in my career that was not an option. I wanted to play Test cricket and to qualify for England, and that was the firm decision I took. There was no other choice once I had decided that a professional approach was the best thing for my future. All my close friends agree with my decision, and so far no one in Zimbabwe (apart from Dave Ellman-Brown in 1986) has told me to my face that I was out of order in throwing in my lot with England. At the time of my decision Zimbabwe's cricket was in a stronger state than it is now, but I wasn't optimistic even then about my country's elevation to Test status. A few years later, I'm even less optimistic.

At present the base, in terms of good players, is not strong enough to build a Test-class squad in Zimbabwe. There never really was after Independence in 1980. Before then, the quality was fairly high as Rhodesia played in the Currie Cup, against the best players in South Africa. Men like John Shepherd, Barry Duddleston and Mike Procter did a lot for Rhodesian cricket, and the likes of Tony Pithey, Colin Bland and John Traicos represented South Africa in the sixties and seventies when South Africa had a very strong side. By 1980, we were out of the Currie Cup for political reasons and there is little prospect of that changing for the moment. Whatever the sport, to maintain and improve standards you need to progress against others at international level and that hasn't really happened for Zimbabwe in the 1980s. At one stage the national side was winning the important international games and so the team didn't really change for about five years for the understandable reason that the selectors wanted to keep a winning combination. So Zimbabwe fell between two stools – wanting to keep the best players happy and not giving themselves the opportunity to blood too many youngsters. For most of the season, the top players in Zimbabwe would end up playing each other in the league and that's no good for anybody – it was all too familiar. So the younger ones left to study in South Africa and play a higher standard of cricket. It got to the stage when several players of limited ability were managing to stay in the Zimbabwe side by the skin of their teeth and by the time a change was contemplated the domestic season was more or less over. I was lucky to get the breaks at the right time, but not many others of my age group got the same opportunity. Some good schoolboys are still coming through but an outstanding prospect today would have been average five or six years ago. There just isn't the depth of talent, and Zimbabwe's selectors can look at no more than forty candidates.

When we made such a good impression in the World Cup in 1983, there was a lot of speculation about us getting Test status, but I don't believe we had the pool of players to sustain the challenge. A lot of the top Zimbabwe players at that time were around thirty and after a couple of Test series they would have retired and very little would have been coming through from the younger ones. In 1986, the team that won the ICC Trophy had some fine players and they carried on to give a good account of themselves in the World Cup the following year. By then, Kevin Curran and I had decided to sever our connections with the national side, but players like David Houghton, John Traicos, Peter Rawson, Andy Pycroft, Grant Paterson and Eddo Brandes comprised the nucleus of a good unit. Yet they weren't professional enough, through no real fault of their own. Some of them just didn't practise hard or often enough to sustain the standards required for first-class cricket. They needed to find well-paid jobs, so that they could stay in Harare to concentrate on improving their game. The money wasn't good enough – in fact it was non-existent at that time.

Even today David Houghton is the only professional cricketer in Zimbabwe.

So if the Zimbabwe Cricket Union wants to keep its top players in the country, they somehow have to find the cash incentives to keep them, and even then they'd be short of the sponsorship deals that are so attractive to the professional cricketer in other parts of the world. This is not meant to sound like money-grabbing, more a reason for the absence of a professional attitude from many of Zimbabwe's best players. You can't blame guys for simply enjoying their cricket, coming to Harare at the weekend after a hard working week on the farm and relaxing with a game or two and a few beers. The need to practise hard isn't inbred in them, so they won't commit themselves a hundred per cent to their cricket. It'll be interesting to see how Grant and Andy Flowers progress as batsmen. Andy plays a bit of cricket in Holland, but apart from that he and his brother play against the same guys every year. They are both talented and young enough to make a career out of cricket, but you can only assess your ability by the quality of the opposition. They are not being stretched enough in Zimbabwe, I'm afraid.

Under the current situation in Zimbabwe, cricket could take off only if the black population gets more interested and involved. Out of a population of ten million, there are only about 90,000 whites still living in Zimbabwe, so cricket at present is just ingrained in a tiny minority. The non-whites prefer soccer to cricket – that's a game that comes naturally to them. Recently, the ZCU have put a black club into the league's first division and I thought that was not the best way to encourage them. They were outclassed in every game, because they were so inexperienced, and that can't have been good for their morale. They would have enjoyed it more if they'd won a few games in a lower division: I can't see them coming back for more, season after season, if they keep getting slaughtered. No one likes that. The next generation of blacks will have to be the ones who take to cricket. They need to be brought up by their parents to love the game, to watch their fathers play at weekends and to decide to do the same.

At the moment, the signs aren't good. They don't seem to be

able to pick up the game as easily as soccer. When I coached some black youngsters a few years ago, I felt sorry for them. We stood in a dust bowl, trying to grasp the basics of a bowling action, and it was hard going. It took me an hour to place marks on the run-up, so that they knew where to land the left foot, then the right foot. So then it was a case of getting to the bowling crease and turning the arm over. They all concentrated hard and it was very important to them to do well. I realised that the worst thing to do was put any one of them down in front of the group; those who hadn't got it right were subjected to mocking laughter by the rest of the boys and that led to sulks. If they got the whole thing right, you could see the pleasure it gave them. One chap brought home to me how difficult it was to coach something that was foreign to the majority of black kids. He managed to get to the crease in the approved fashion, but then he did a 360-degree turn before delivering the ball. It looked so bizarre and it was hard not to laugh, but hardly any of them had seen proper bowlers at a cricket match, because they never went to games. If you had asked any of them how to pass a football or how to tackle properly, that would have been no problem.

Somehow the game of cricket has to be brought to the black community; perhaps more tours by the West Indies would help, but where will the ZCU find the money to attract Viv Richards and the others? The President of Zimbabwe, Robert Mugabe, is a big cricket fan and publicly pleads with non-whites to get more involved in the game, but more sponsorship and coaching are vital to spread the word in the black townships. Zimbabwe isn't a rich country. There is a massive shortage of cricket equipment, and it's very hard even to buy a decent bat. For a time, a manufacturer tried to make bats that were made out of a soft wood, but it was like picking up a piece of wood torn from a fence. They were useless and only highlighted the difficulty in getting the right gear to play the game properly.

It's a chicken-and-egg situation, this desire to get Zimbabwe into Test cricket. On the one hand, the standards can only improve if the top international teams come out regularly to Zimbabwe. That happened when New Zealand, India and Pakistan first played Test cricket; they had to take their thrashings and wait for decades before the competition hardened up their players. The same hopefully would apply to Zimbabwe, except that there isn't a bottomless pit of enthusiasm among the vast majority of the country's population. Cricket might just fade away in Zimbabwe, unless the game's administrators there feel they are getting enough encouragement in their efforts to enter Test cricket. Yet if that happened I doubt if there would be tremendous interest at the start of Zimbabwe's Test history. The side made its name in one-day internationals in the 1980s and hardly anyone is interested in the longer game – it's just not snappy enough for them. If a world eleven came to Zimbabwe to play a series of games, I doubt if more than 15,000 would turn up to watch – and that would include a lot who had come up from South Africa to watch the world's best players in action. The crowds for the England A matches early in 1990 were pitifully thin when they played a first-class match: they were lucky to attract about 800, and that included many schoolchildren who were allowed in free.

Yet Zimbabwe's cricketers desperately need top-class competition and they're not really getting it. There's a big difference between an English county side going out there for some gentle pre-season practice and coming up against world-class players once every four years when the World Cup comes around. It looks as if Zimbabwe will keep qualifying for those World Cups because they are still the best one-day side among the ICC countries, but it would be unrealistic to assume that that means they should be knocking on the Test match door. In my time in the game, Zimbabwe has never been all that strong in the longer game: they have been one-day specialists. So their performances are unrealistic when it comes to assessing how they would do in five-day Tests.

After the England A team showed far greater professionalism in the series in Zimbabwe, the home captain David Houghton admitted that the series had shown that they were now lagging far behind and that the gap was getting bigger. The average age in the Zimbabwe team was now up to twenty-nine, and in the absence of a first-class domestic programme it is hard to see how the established players can improve. Alwyn Pichanick and Dave Ellman-Brown, who have worked so hard over the years for the Zimbabwe Cricket Union, are right to keep pushing the claims for Test status by arguing that it would halt the exodus of top players and also persuade the government to plough more funds into developing the game. For their sakes, and for men like John Traicos – who has been a brilliant ambassador for Zimbabwe cricket – it would be wonderful to see the Test door open. But too many factors are conspiring against the dream – most of them beyond the influence of these sincere men. I would be thrilled to see Zimbabwe playing Test cricket – but I shall be surprised if that happens in the foreseeable future.

CHAPTER SIXTEEN

England Expects

NOW that I have finally qualified for England, I know that I will be fair game for all sorts of knocking publicity. I have to get runs in the early part of the season to force my way into contention and if that doesn't happen, some will say 'What's wrong with Hick?' If I do get picked for England, and I fail initially, many will say, 'I told you so, there's a big gap between the county game and Test matches.' As if I wasn't aware of that! If I manage to do well, I don't suppose it will then be a big deal, because my batting record has been fairly satisfactory so far and the pundits will state that I was always destined to be a Test-class batsman. It's so easy to be wise after the event. I'm quite relaxed about all the possible permutations – there's nothing much I can do about it and I'm determined not to go on about being 'under pressure'. At this stage in my career, I *want* such a challenge. Challenges always seem to present themselves just when I need an extra stimulus and they don't come much more exciting than going for an England place, with the West Indies as the opposition.

I suppose the hardest thing to get over will be the expectancy, but I think I can handle that. Graham Gooch started his Test career with a 'pair' and he hasn't been a bad player. I know that if I get in the team I shan't walk out there, score a hundred and then keep getting them for England. If I manage to play Test cricket, I will give myself two years before I can assess whether I've got it in me to be a Test batsman. Obviously I back myself to do so, but there are many hurdles I haven't yet encountered and it's uncharted territory for me. I've made a point of watching more and more Test cricket on the television in recent years, just to familiarise myself as much as possible, but there are many aspects about it that you just have to experience for yourself. I'm not the kind of person to take a current England player to one side and quiz him all about it, so I'll wait to see if I can force my way in and then take it steadily, step by step. That's why I believe I need about four series over a couple of years before I could judge my progress. It took Mike Gatting and Graham Gooch long enough to come to terms with the demands of Test cricket and I don't expect to take to it like a duck to water. It would help if I got picked for the one-day internationals before the Test series starts; the wickets for those games are often pretty flat and with hardly anyone around the bat there's less chance of getting caught early on. Besides, the bowlers look to contain in those type of matches, compared to the Test when the West Indies in particular put pressure on the batters with short-pitched fast bowling and close fielders.

I am sure it will be said that I still have to prove myself against consistent short-pitched fast bowling, something that will be almost ever-present against the West Indies. As far as I'm concerned, I have seen a fair bit of that during my time in county cricket: not every wicket I've played on in England has been as dead as most of those in the 1990 season. I talked about this with Basil D'Oliveira last year. I asked him if I should look to play more off the back foot, in preparation for the stuff you often encounter in Tests. Basil was his usual forthright self – 'What for? What do you do best? You bat naturally. Don't change that.' He pointed out that I hadn't done too badly against the West Indies in May 1988 when I scored 172 on a pitch that was far from straightforward and I must keep telling myself that. I know I have the patience to sway out of line if they try to get me bobbing and weaving; you don't have to have played Test cricket to know that it's also a test of mental steel, to be able to curb your strokes and battle through to a time when batting is easier and you can capitalise. That's something I think I can do. I know I have to be very tough mentally, but I have a great desire to survive if I get the chance.

The longer my career has lasted, the greater has been my need to make something of it. So I have tried to assess when I should train hard and when I should relax and switch off from cricket. You have to be very strong mentally to continue succeeding in first-class cricket;

once you get to such a standard, it's assumed you have the natural ability and then it's a case of seeing how far you can go. I have been interested to see how the established England players have had to live with speculation about their Test careers, about how near they are to being dropped, and I find myself imagining what it will be like coping with that kind of media exercise. Last summer I couldn't believe how many were writing off the England career of David Gower. He is just about my favourite player; if I knew he was going to score a hundred for England I would want to be there that day, because of the style and grace he brings to the game. He has a proven Test record yet I kept reading that it was 'Do or Die for Gower' each time he was due to bat. I thought that was ridiculous and I really admired the way he kept his composure. What was even more impressive was the way he cemented his place in the England side by playing his own natural game. He was strong enough not to alter the approach that has brought him sixteen Test hundreds and an average of more than 40 over the past twelve years. He knew that his natural method was the best one for him. That is something I shan't alter. I'll just have to stick with the method that's served me well since 1984, when I altered my stance at the crease.

I am sure there will be quite a few folk who will say, 'He shouldn't be playing for England' whether or not I do well. Robin Smith and Allan Lamb have faced the same attitude for the past few years – yet, strangely enough, it seems to me that there aren't so many complaints about the fast bowlers from the Caribbean who now play for England. Would it have made any difference if I had come over to England a few years earlier than seventeen? Some of the current England players who were born abroad spent some time getting their education away from England, so it's a case of six of one and half a dozen of the other. I can't win with those whose minds are made up, but to the fair-minded ones I can only say that I will have fulfilled the residential requirements and done all that was required of me. Since 1984 I have done everything to fulfil my qualification towards playing for England and I am very excited about proving myself in a higher league, as long as I get the chance.

I know that many England players get jaded after a few years, that the prospect of playing in Pakistan or on flat Indian wickets doesn't appeal as it used to do, but for my part I would love the chance to play under so many different conditions. For a professional cricketer, I can't think of anything more demanding than coming to terms with Abdul Qadir spinning the ball prodigiously at Lahore, then next year fending off the West Indies quickies in the Caribbean, followed by a tour to New Zealand where the wickets are slower. Then walking out to bat in front of 90,000 people at the Melbourne Cricket Ground with the Ashes at stake – that must be a great thrill even for the most experienced cricketer. I know I want to be a part of that, beginning with playing in a Test at Lord's, the most famous ground in the world. For years I have daydreamed about the chance to play Test cricket at Lord's and I just trust I can make it happen.

I hope I shall remain the same person whatever happens to me. I honestly don't think I'm the type who gets carried away by success. For many, I suspect that the hard thing is that everything seems to step up a gear when you suddenly become a household name and so many people want a piece of you. For me, I really don't see that as a problem. If a sports personality withdraws into himself and becomes a virtual recluse, then it is inevitable that his public appearances are an event. You bring those sort of problems on yourself. In my case, I like walking down the main street in Worcester, doing my shopping and saying 'hello' to people who recognise me. It doesn't take much to stop and smile when someone says 'Hello, good luck tomorrow.' In almost every case, they mean well and that deserves a polite response. I'll say, 'Thank you, have a nice day,' and be on my way, without any bother. I also like walking around the ground at Worcester, where you can meet all sorts of interesting characters, who have different views about the cricket and don't put you on a pedestal. It can be difficult if you go into a sponsor's tent and you come up against people who suddenly get tongue-tied and don't know what to say. On other occasions, a genuine cricket fan will prattle on about something so much that you get embarrassed for him and think, 'I'll have a pint of what he's been drinking,' but it has never been a hassle for me.

Since 1988, when I had such a good season at Worcester, I have got used to being recognised, but the vast majority of folk are very nice. If you are normal and unaffected, the ordinary person soon realises you are genuine; I would hate it if someone didn't want to say 'hello' because they thought I was somebody special and therefore unapproachable. As a shy individual myself, I know how words and actions can be misunderstood and the only time I get annoyed is when rude people throw bits of paper at me and expect me to autograph them without even a polite request. Even now I won't go to a bar on my own unless I know I'm meeting a friend there; I like to feel secure in my environment, to feel that I'm not out of my depth. I'm sure the likes of Boris Becker, John McEnroe and Ian Botham would love to walk down a street without being hassled, but they would be the first to acknowledge that though being famous has its disadvantages, it does open a few doors. My success in 1988 helped me become more confident as a person and I admit that I like it when I walk around in Worcester and hear someone whisper, 'Look, there's Graeme Hick.' To me that means I have done something in my life that some folk consider notable, and it's a nice feeling.

If I fail initially in Test cricket, I'll be relying on the Worcestershire players and Basil D'Oliveira to pick me up when I get back to New Road. Much the same will apply if I do well. I just know there'll be no danger of getting big ideas with that lot around me. They can soon deflate you if you think you're somebody special. I hope they realise that I shall be trying my hardest for my county whatever happens on the international scene. If I manage to play for England and it goes well, it will be partly due to the advice and backing I have had at New Road since 1984, so I owe it to them – as well as to myself – to maintain my standards. There will be no coasting though the county matches from me. I am too hungry for runs and more county trophies for that.

There will be even less danger of being put on a pedestal back in Zimbabwe. Just because there will be a lot of family and friends flying out from Harare for my first game for England if I am selected doesn't mean I'm seen as some sort of superstar over there.

Zimbabwe isn't a media-conscious country and although some follow my progress on the radio through the World Service it's no big deal when Graeme Hick comes back to Trelawney. I wouldn't have it any other way; I get even more leg-pulling when I go back than when I was setting up records at Prince Edward's School. Even if I somehow developed big ideas, my parents would soon pull me back into line, quickly followed by my sister Sharon and Mike my brother-in-law. As a family we don't get carried away – the others are delighted for me, but I never forget that I wasn't the only talented person at sport in our family. When I go back to Zimbabwe I stay with my close friends and just enjoy their company. I've never been one to force myself on to others if I don't know them, so I keep clear of anything that might suggest I pose around, thinking I've really got it made.

I honestly believe that, apart from gaining some self-confidence, I haven't changed all that much – and that was why I threatened to sue the *Sunday Times* for libel in the spring of 1990. A chap called Martin Searby wrote an article about me for that paper, in which he suggested that I had got too big for my boots and that many people in Zimbabwe were fed up with me. The article was headlined 'Hick's good-guy image under fire' and it was pretty strong stuff. He said that I no longer bothered to go back to my old school and help out with coaching, that I swaggered through the Harare Sports Club as if I owned the place and that I hadn't paid my debt to my country. Well, the only thing Searby got right is that I was regularly seen on the balcony at the Sports Club picking my toes – a regular fault, I am afraid. I have in fact done a lot of coaching at Prince Edward's – indeed I spent an afternoon there not long before Searby's article appeared in print. I have helped out whenever I have been asked and I'm in the country – not that regular an occurrence any more. I have done all sorts of things for Zimbabwean cricket that I needn't go on about – except to state that I have never charged any money for them. Searby also alleged that my parents were thinking of emigrating to Worcester, so that Dad could manage my business affairs. That was nonsense; he has never thought of doing either; he has his hands full on the tobacco farm, and Mum and Dad have far too many roots and close friends in the Trelawney area for them ever to think about moving anywhere. Searby also called me 'an idiot', which I thought a bit stiff. He had never met my parents before that article appeared and typically the quotes knocking me were anonymous.

The background to the article is important. When my Worcester team-mates Steve Rhodes and Richard Illingworth arrived in Zimbabwe early in 1990 with England's A team, I obviously looked them up on their first night. Along with my girlfriend Jackie and Eddo Brandes, a good friend from the days when I played for Zimbabwe, we went for a drink at the Harare Sports Club. When we got there, a few guys who had had too much to drink made whistling sounds at Jackie and offered a few choice comments about her. I wasn't too impressed by that, but decided to keep a low profile and the five of us went out on to the balcony for a quiet drink. Searby, whom I had already seen with a couple of other English reporters I knew in the bar, came up to me on the balcony and was rather rude. He asked for an interview; I agreed to one but when he mentioned the next day I said I couldn't, because I had made other commitments. He then said his interview was also for the BBC, as well as for a newspaper, as if that would have made any difference. I said politely that I'd be at the game on the Sunday – this conversation took place on the Friday night – and I'd be happy to talk then. He wasn't happy at all about that and went away. Steve Rhodes said, 'Well done, Hicky, some of those blokes think they can just order us around,' but I wasn't rude to Searby. I just stood up for myself as well as making it perfectly clear that I'd talk to him on the Sunday.

When the article appeared, I was very annoyed at the allegations about my parents. I was even more annoyed about that than when he called me an idiot who was abusing his talent. Eventually the *Sunday Times* printed an apology, withdrew the allegations and agreed to pay me damages. The point about the whole incident is not only that Searby's article was full of inaccuracies, but that it stemmed from the fact that he obviously felt I had been unhelpful to him. I don't believe I was.

I hope that if I do have a decent Test career, I won't get many hassles like that one. It hasn't changed my view of the media. I shall continue trying to be co-operative with them, because that is

159

a branch of professionalism in cricket. There is no point in having vendettas against certain sections of the media; if you don't like their opinions, you should accept that and forget it. There's no need for any of them to be on your Christmas card list, but I feel that if you let adverse criticism get to you, then you are being a little weak in character. I play cricket for my team, for my self-respect, but also for the respect of my colleagues, and their opinions matter more to me than someone seated in a press box. I believe you get out of a sport what you put in. I like to think that if I changed my sport and concentrated on golf, then I would get my handicap down to scratch and have a crack at the game as a professional. I say that in the knowledge that it's a very difficult sport, but also believing that if you really want something desperately, then you can make it happen. Weakness of character lets too many people down; the successful ones have stacks of self-belief, a positive attitude and a desire to work hard. I now have a real desire to do well in my chosen profession. It's so important to be consistent in top-class sport – natural ability just isn't enough.

I don't want to leave the game having played just a handful of Tests and unable to bridge the gap between success at county level and the real top drawer. I'm the kind of chap who wants to do something well once I decide to have a crack at it, and when I retire from first-class cricket I hope that I shall leave some kind of a mark. I've had a very good grounding in the professional game at Worcester, and my qualification period has given me breathing space, time to work out various matters that could have caused me grief if I had been thrown to the wolves early on in Test cricket. Basil D'Oliveira's advice on the mental side of the game has been valuable, and he has been brilliant at how to handle the media and how to prepare for an innings. Now I want to go up a stage, to play Test cricket. I don't want to be any old Test player – I want to succeed, but that is something for the future. If hard work and professionalism are major factors, then I'm on my way. If I get some luck and keep approaching my career positively, then I've got a chance. I think I can honestly say I'm now ready for the next, and biggest, challenge of my career.

Statistical Appendices

Compiled by Robert Brooke, Association of Cricket Statisticians

Graeme Hick in first-class cricket: season-by-season record

Season	Mch	Inn	N.o.	Runs	H.s.	Av'ge	100s	50s	Ct	Overs	Mdns	Runs	Wts	Av'ge	5inn	10mch
1983/84	6	11	2	190	57	21.11	–	1	10	65	18	169	3	56.33	–	–
1984	1	1	1	82	82*	–	–	1	1	6	0	27	0	–	–	–
1984/5	6	12	1	389	95	35.36	–	2	5	82	12	312	7	44.57	–	–
1985	17	25	1	1265	230	52.70	4	3	12	146	27	501	8	62.62	–	–
1985/6	3	5	0	332	154	66.40	2	–	5	18	5	43	0	–	–	–
1986	24	37	6	2004	227*	64.64	6	11	29	28.4	5	109	3	36.33	–	–
1987	25	38	2	1879	173	52.19	8	6	13	310.2	59	1042	25	41.68	–	–
1987/8	9	14	1	827	146	63.61	4	3	9	71	24	137	2	68.50	–	–
1988	24	37	2	2713	405*	77.51	10	5	28	204	43	642	21	30.57	–	–
1988/9	8	16	3	1228	211*	94.46	6	2	8	20	10	46	1	–	–	1
1989	24	38	6	1824	173*	57.00	6	8	43	214.4	65	519	26	19.96	2	–
1990	21	35	9	2347	252*	90.26	8	14	26	208.5	41	645	20	32.25	1	–
Total	168	269	34	15080	405*	64.17	54	56	189	1374.3	309	4192	116	36.13	3	1

Note: *nk* – not known; *cw* – caught at the wicket; *m* – minutes; *b* – balls received; *ro* – run out.

Graeme Hick in first-class cricket: innings by innings

Match	Runs	Dismissal	Mins	Balls	4s	6s	Other Notes
1983/84							
Z v. Young WI, Harare	28*		80	nk	4	–	F-c debut age
	12	b C.Butts	31	nk	1	–	17 yrs 137days
Z v. Young WI, Harare	12	cw b C.Walsh	29	nk	2	–	
	4*		1	1	1	–	
Z v. Sri Lanka Pres. XI, Moratuwa	4	b Amerasinghe	32	35	1	–	
Z v. Sri Lanka, Colombo	9	ro	33	28	1	–	
	57	st b Ranatunga	172	125	6	–	50: 162 m
Z v. Young India, Harare	23	b Kulkarni	91	nk	2	–	
	15	cw b Prabhakar	86	nk	2	–	
Z v. Young India, Harare	18	c b Maninder	39	nk	1	–	
	8	b Maninder	87	nk	–	–	
1984							
W v. Surrey, Oval	82*		106	110	8	3	50: 80m 48b
1984/5							
Z v. Young NZ, Harare	8	c M. Sneddon	14	14	2	–	
	23	c V. Brown	73	74	3	1	
Z v. Young NZ, Bulawayo	0	c V. Brown	16	10	–	–	
	30	ro	30	22	6	–	
Z v. Young NZ, Harare	95	lbw J. Bracewell	127	105	17	–	50: 83m
	22	lbw V. Brown	52	59	1	–	
Z v. Young NZ, Harare	88	cw G. Robertson	136	136	15	–	50: 84m
	38*		112	66	5	–	
Z v. Eng. Cos., Harare	42	cw P. Newman	101	nk	4	–	
	6	lbw N. Cook	9	nk	–	–	
Z v. Eng. Cos., Harare	14	st N. Cook	59	nk	2	–	
	23	c N. Williams	35	nk	4	–	
1985							
W v. OU, Ox.	3	c M. Lawrence	21	18	–	–	
Z v. OU, Ox.	230	b D. Thorne	294	nk	31	4	50: 98m
							100: 149m
							150: 211m
							200: 268m
Z v. Glam., Swansea	192	c M.R. Price	243	nk	22	3	50: 90m
							100: 138m
							150: 209m
Z v. Warks, Edgbaston	4	b S. Wall	4	nk	1	–	
	65	c A. Pierson	65	nk	11	1	50: 60m
Z v. Minor Cos., Cleethorpes	19	cw K. Arnold	25	nk	2	–	
	38	c T. Smith	104	nk	8	–	
Z v. Surrey, Oval	10	lbw P. Waterman	20	nk	2	–	
Z v. Glos., Bristol	1	cw G. Sainsbury	7	nk	–	–	
	39	c P. Twizell	60	nk	7	–	
W v. Sussex, Eastbourne	22	b A. Pigott	84	67	2	–	
	35	b D. Reeve	34	45	1	1	
W. v. Notts, Trent B	20	c R. Hadlee	26	25	4	–	
	10	c P. Such	21	23	2	–	
W v. Derby, Buxton	–						
W v. Essex, Worc.	56	b N. Foster	153	100	9	–	50: 136m, 89b
W v. Warks, Edgbaston	3	b G. Small	5	5	–	–	
	62	c D. Hoffmann	96	94	8	2	50: 82m, 84b
W v. Kent, Worc.	35	b D. Underwood	84	77	5	–	
	47	b L. Potter	79	74	9	–	
W v. Leics, Le'ster	21	b P. Willey	64	50	2	–	
W v. Som., Worc.	174*		268	243	24	2	50: 120m, 94b
							100: 184m, 156b
	2	b C. Dredge	27	23	2	–	

Match	Runs	Dismissal	Mins	Balls	4s	6s	Other Notes
W v. Som., Taunton	38	c R. Coombs	86	86	5	–	
W v. N'hants, Worc.	129	c D. Capel	214	182	19	1	50: 94m, 77b
							100: 160m, 144b
	12	b D. Capel	27	23	2	–	
1985/6							
Z v. Young Aust., Harare	127	lbw R. Brown	208	nk	21	–	50: 98m
							100: 176m
Z v. Young Aust., Harare	7	c D. Gilbert	29	nk	1	–	
	154	c D. Gilbert	250	nk	18	1	50: 98m
							100: 152m
							150: 237m
Z v. Young NSW, Harare	40	cw R. Done	79	80	8	–	
	4	c M. Whitney	2	4	1	–	
1986							
W v. Surrey, Worc.	5	b S. Clarke	9	9	1	–	
	103	cw S. Clarke	186	145	15	3	50: 86m, 72b
							100: 184m, 182b
W v. Indians, Worc.	70	c Maninder	137	123	10	1	50: 91m, 89b
W v. Lancs, Worc.	18	lbw D. Makinson	47	40	2	–	
W v. Warks, Edgbaston	62	c G. Parsons	57	60	9	1	50: 49m, 50b
	53	b N. Gifford	83	99	7	–	50: 73m, 84b
W v. Kent, Tunbridge W	–						
W v. M'sex, Worc.	70	c S. Hughes	101	117	15	–	50: 84m, 76b
W v. N'hants, No'ton	39	cw N. Cook	75	73	4	–	
	1	c J. Griffiths	10	8	–	–	
W v. Lancs, O Trafford	13	st M. Watkinson	40	30	1	–	
	9	ro	17	9	2	–	
W v. Yorks, Worc.	36*		27	39	3	1	
	60	cw N. Hartley	102	75	8	1	50: 92m, 69b
W v. Hants, Worc.	21	c M. Marshall	54	46	3	–	
	0	b M. Marshall	14	9	–	–	
W v. Derby, Derby	94	c M. Jean-Jacques	184	146	13	–	50: 108m, 83b
W v. Notts, Worc.	0	cw R. Hadlee	8	5	–	–	
	227*		288	303	31	5	50: 90m, 90b
							100: 191m, 197b
							150: 239m, 241b
							200: 284m, 293b
W v. Glam., Neath	219*		172	146	25	8	50: 57m, 45b
							100: 105m, 85b
							150: 136m, 114b
							200: 160m, 137b
	52	c R. Ontong	25	22	6	3	50: 24m, 21b
W v. Essex, Southend	51	c J. Lever	64	48	10	–	50: 64m, 47b
	29	b D. Pringle	49	43	4	–	
W v. Sussex, Hove	4	c G. Le Roux	7	6	1	–	
	100	c N. Lenham	136	103	13	1	50: 92m, 73b
							100: 133m, 102b
W v. Glos., Worc.	4*		7	2	1	–	
	134	cw D. Graveney	212	178	16	–	50: 125m, 96b
					(+1	.5)	100: 165m, 136b
W v. Som., Weston	30	cw R. Coombs	74	66	4	–	
	43*		30	36	1	5	
W v. Surrey, Oval	31	b K. Medlycott	56	61	4	–	
W v. Leics, Worc.	45*		98	99	7	–	
	34	cw L. Taylor	34	40	6	–	
W v. Hants, B'mouth	0	cw M. Marshall	3	2	–	–	
	81	c R. Maru	111	109	15	–	50: 66m, 74b
W v. Warks, Worc.	–						
W v. Glos., Bristol	85	c C. Walsh	85	84	11	–	50: 58m, 57b
W v. Som., Worc.	13	b C. Dredge	30	31	1	–	
W v. Glam., Worc.	61	c S. Watkin	77	76	10	1	50: 71m, 71b
	107	c S. Barwick	152	126	8		50: 100m, 80b
							100: 147m, 121b

Match	Runs	Dismissal	Mins	Balls	4s	6s	Other Notes
1987							
W v. Kent, Worc.	29	c D. Underwood	58	47	6	–	
	68	lbw K. Jarvis	107	72	8	2	50: 65m, 46b
W v. Sussex, Worc.	107	lbw G. Le Roux	199	178	16	1	50: 117m, 89b
							100: 181m, 173b
	23	b A. Wells	26	34	4	–	
W v. Derby, Worc.	37	c A. Warner	46	49	5	–	
	41	c A. Warner	30	23	3	3	
W v. Lancs, O Trafford	0	cw P. Allott	1	1	–	–	
	11	st I. Folley	10	11	1	1	
W v. Essex, Worc.	29	cw N. Foster	88	72	5	–	
	1	c N. Foster	4	3	–	–	
W v. Yorks, Sheff.	54	c P. Carrick	63	60	9	1	50: 59m, 56b
W v. Leics, Le'ster	16*		27	23	1	1	
W v. Leics, Worc.	1	lbw J. Agnew	10	7	–	–	
W v. Glos., Worc.	–						
W v. Notts, Trent B	2	cw R. Hadlee	7	10	–	–	
	69	c M. Newell	95	96	9	1	50: 75m, 75b
W v. Glos., Glo'ster	138	cw J. Lloyds	239	233	16	2	50: 95m, 81b
							100: 200m, 186b
	24	lbw C. Walsh	59	36	5	–	
W v. Notts, Kidderm'r	63	lbw A. Pick	105	93	10	–	50: 86m, 79b
W v. Warks, Worc.	19	lbw T. Munton	33	33	4	–	
	0	cw A. Donald	2	2	–	–	
W v. Som., Taunton	0	b V. Marks	12	11	–	–	
W v. Pakis, Worc.	11	b Mudassar	74	55	–	–	
W v. Surrey, Oval	30	lbw I. Greig	51	35	4	–	
W v. Som., Worc.	132	c V. Marks	251	186	17	1	50: 85m, 58b
							100: 184m, 128b
	29	c A.N. Jones	19	19	6	–	
W v. M'sex, Lord's	173	b W. Daniel	305	245	19	0	50: 107m, 94b
							100: 178m, 157b
							150: 240m, 203b
	4	lbw N. Cowans	12	10	–	–	
W v. Glam., Worc.	34	cw I. Smith	79	78	5	–	
W v. N'hants, No'ton	87	c A. Walker	144	13	2	–	50: 113m, 97b
	107	lbw R. Williams	169	150	16	–	50: 83m, 76b
							100: 162m, 140b
W v. Glam., Neath	32	c P. North	44	42	5	–	
	9	st P. North	24	26	–	1	
W v. Hants, Worc.	5	c R. Maru	17	20	–	–	
	16	b T. Tremlett	58	38	3	–	
W v. Warks, Edgbaston	126	c T. Munton	232	206	17	1	50: 117m, 88b
							100: 180m, 163b
W v. Essex, Colchester	156	c J. Stephenson	253	207	19	1	50: 94m, 75b
							100: 186m, 154b
							150: 247m, 200b
W v. N'hants, Worc.	140*		175	183	20	1	50: 75m, 68b
							100: 139m, 145b
	56	c N. Cook	60	51	7	1	50: 54m, 46b
1987/8							
ND v. Wellington, Hamilton	0	c J. Millmow	3	3	–	–	
	64	b E. Gray	114	117	6	1	
ND v. Canterbury, Christchurch	7	b M. Priest	24	23	–	–	
	113*		81	97	15	4	50: 34m
							100: 77m, 94b
ND v. Otago, Alexandra	4	b S. Boock	31	22	–	–	
	90	lbw T.J. Wilson	128	106	13	2	
ND v. Central Dists, Te Awamutu	27	c T. McKenna	55	41	5	–	
ND v. England XI, Hamilton	19	c D. Capel	57	36	4	–	
	146	c E. Hemmings	185	152	14	7	
ND v. Otago, Hamilton	122	c B. Blair	195	190	16	1	100: 177m, 176b

Match	Runs	Dismissal	Mins	Balls	4s	6s	Other Notes
ND v. Auckland, Auckland	6	c M. Snedden	37	25	1	–	
	26	c M. Snedden	60	42	5	–	
ND v. Central D, Palmerston N	62	b S. Duff	80	75	12	–	
ND v. Auckland, Hamilton	141	c W.P. Fowler	224	192	13	3	100: 181m, 169b
1988							
MCC v. Notts, Lord's	61	c A. Pick		74			
	37	c A. Pick					
W v. Lancs, O Trafford	212	b J. Simmons	345	312	25	4	50: 91m, 85b
							100: 179m, 149b
							150: 263m, 249b
							200: 327m, 292b
W v. Notts, Worc.	86	c K. Cooper	114	106	12	4	50: 83m, 77b
	14	cw F. Stephenson	24	22	2	–	
W v. Som., Taunton	405*		553	469	35	11	50: 81m, 59b
							100: 153m, 126b
							150: 244m, 194b
							200: 342m, 278b
							250: 403m, 334b
							300: 484m, 411b
							350: 529m, 441b
							400: 553m, 469b
W v. Som., Worc.	8	c A. Jones	11	10	2	–	
	11	c A.N. Jones	22	19	2	–	
W v. Leics, Le'ster	6	b G. Ferris	10	16	1	–	
	7	b C. Lewis	16	10	1	–	
W v. W Indians, Worc.	172	cw P. Patterson	345	270	25	–	50: 170m, 119b
							100: 267m, 194b
							150: 326m, 252b
W v. Lancs, Worc.	0	c A. Hayhurst	7	6	–	–	
	8	cw P. Allott	24	16	1	–	
W v. M'sex, Lord's	78	b S. Hughes	120	92	12	–	50: 70m, 55b
W v. Hants, Worc.	177	cw N. Cowley	265	223	19	2	50: 97m, 78b
							100: 186m, 153b
							150: 239m, 203b
W v. Derby, Derby	47	c B. Roberts	72	58	8	–	
	31	lbw R. Sharma	29	34	4	–	
W v. Glos., Worc.	20	b T. Alderman	58	37	3	–	
W v. Warks, Edgbaston	23	b A. Pierson	43	33	5	–	
W v. Notts, Trent B	8	lbw K. Cooper	34	22	1	–	
	76	cw K. Evans	146	111	8	1	50: 99m, 77b
W v. Yorks, Worc.	198	c C. Shaw	277	227	23	2	50: 71m, 59b
							100: 148m, 124b
							150: 220m, 182b
	17	b P. Carrick	25	26	3	–	
W v. Kent, Folkestone	21	c R. Ellison	57	21	3	–	
W v. N'hants, Worc.	132	cw M. Robinson	183	155	16	1	50: 80m, 60b
							100: 138m, 112b
W v. Sussex, Kidderm'r	18	c A. Babbington	49	43	2	–	
	2*		5	3	–	–	
W v. Glam., Abergavenny	46	b G. Holmes	92	76	6	–	
	159	c S. Watkin	222	186	15	5	50: 99m, 83b
							100: 175m, 152b
							150: 211m, 178b
W v. Surrey, Oval	41	cw K. Medlycott	80	49	6	1	
	127	c J. Robinson	98	88	12	5	50: 56m, 41b
							100: 91m, 79b
W v. Essex, Worc.	34	c T. Topley	60	50	7	–	
	20	c D. Pringle	39	35	3	–	
W v. Warks, Worc.	75	c N. Gifford	175	141	12	–	50: 119m, 96b
W v. Glos., Bristol	121	b D. Graveney	212	172	17	2	50: 84m, 63b
							100: 180m, 149b
	18	lbw D. Lawrence	36	26	3	–	

Match	Runs	Dismissal	Mins	Balls	4s	6s	Other Notes
W v. Glam., Worc.	197	c J.G. Thomas	327	263	29	–	50: 91m, 70b
							100: 162m, 124b
							150: 249m, 205b
1988/9							
ND v. C Dists, Napier	57	b S. Duff	136	122	9	–	
	105	b P. Briasco	150	131	13	–	100: 135m, 121b
ND v. Otago, Gisborne	12	c V. Johnson	42	25	3	–	
	44*		68	57	7	1	
ND v. Wellington, Wellington	121*		296	205	19	1	100: 212m, 170b
	1	b F. Beyeler	6	3	–	–	
ND v. Canterbury, Hamilton	145	c M. Robinson	237	199	19	–	100: 173m, 134b
	71	c M. Priest	73	80	6	3	
ND v. Auckland, Auckland	27	cw M. Snedden	84	70	4	–	
	211*		282	241	27	2	100: 182m, 157b
							200: 272m, 234b
ND v. Wellington, Morrinsville	144	cw B. Williams	221	200	17	–	100: 172m, 146b
	132	c T. Ritchie	154	153	12	3	100: 147m, 142b
ND v. Auckland, Hamilton	49	cw P. Neutze	202	145	1	–	
	33	c D. Morrison	34	23	5	–	
ND v. Canterbury, Christchurch	41	b S. Roberts	68	52	6	–	
	35	c M. Priest	37	48	5	–	
1989							
W v. MCC, Lord's	173*		338	237	22	4	50:122m, 94b
							100: 249m, 173b
							150: 299m, 204b
W v. Notts, Trent B	56	lbw K. Cooper	118	86	9	–	50: 96m, 71b
	55*		98	66	7	–	50: 97m, 64b
W v. Warks, Edgbaston	7	c T. Munton	41	30	1	–	
	5	lbw T. Munton	61	11	2	–	
W v. Lancs, Worc.	15	lbw Wasim Akram	57	42	3	–	
	2	c P. DeFreitas	16	7	–	–	
W v. Australians, Worcs.	13	c S. Waugh	63	35	2	–	
	43	c S. Waugh	72	56	9	–	
W v. Notts, Worc.	9	c K. Evans	28	28	2	–	
	90*		79	75	5	7	50: 68m, 60b
W v. Glos., Bristol	8	b D. Lawrence	26	18	1	–	
	53	b D. Graveney	114	82	7	–	50: 111m, 70b
W v. Glam., Worc.	43	lbw S. Barwick	139	112	8	–	
	0	c S. Watkin	5	3	–	–	
W v. Derby, Worc.	17	c P. Newman	46	40	2	–	
	42	cw I. Bishop	37	32	8	–	
W v. Yorks, Sheff.	150	cw C. Pickles	196	156	25	2	50: 80m, 71b
							100: 160m, 122b
							150: 195m, 154b
W v. M'sex, Worc.	5	b A. Fraser	20	12	–	–	
	6	b A. Fraser	11	5	1	–	
W v. N'hants, No'ton	111	cw N. Cook	190	163	16	2	50: 94m, 69b
							100: 175m, 152b
W v. Warks, Worc.	4	b A. Merrick	9	8	1	–	
W v. Leics, Kidderm'r	41	b G. Parsons	66	51	7	–	
W v. Lancs, O Trafford	21	c P. Allott	53	31	4	–	
	16	c N. Watkinson	65	38	2	–	
W v. Sussex, Hove	0	c A. Dodemaide	13	12	–	–	
	110*		170	122	13	3	50: 93m, 74b
							100: 165m, 118b
W v. Surrey, Worc.	9	lbw M. Feltham	39	28	2	–	
	85	lbw K. Medlycott	108	71	14	1	50: 83m, 56b
W v. Kent, Worc.	147	b C. Penn	230	184	14	4	50: 109m, 81b
							100: 188m, 161b
W v. Essex, Colchester	72	c N. Foster	115	112	11	1	50: 84m, 82b
W v. Somerset, Weston	72	lbw V. Marks	126	107	11	–	50: 91m, 72b
	39*		64	54	2	1	

Match	Runs	Dismissal	Mins	Balls	4s	6s	Other Notes
W v. Hants, B'mouth	44	c K. James	88	73	7	1	
W v. Somerset, Worc.	86	c A. Jones	196	147	14	–	50: 106m, 80b
	136*		168	120	10	3	50: 78m, 68b
							100: 129m, 98b
W v. Glos., Worc.	19	lbw K. Curran	26	25	4	–	
	20	c P. Bainbridge	42	26	4	–	
W v. Glamorgan, Pontypridd	–						
1990							
W v. MCC, Lord's	72	c D. Lawrence	154	126	12	–	50: 109m, 98b
W v. Lancs, O Trafford	23	b M. Watkinson	51	41	4	–	
	106*		161	123	10	3	50: 93m, 67b
							100: 138m, 111b
W v. Notts, Worc.	97	b F. Stephenson	229	188	15	–	50: 118m, 105b
W v. N Zealanders, Worc.	2*		25	20	–	–	
W v. Surrey, Oval	59	cw M. Bicknell	98	95	8	–	50: 85m, 81b
W v. Sussex, Worc.	28	cw A. Pigott	49	41	6	–	
W v. M'sex, Lord's	0	b N. Cowans	3	4	–	–	
	80	c P. Tufnell	174	161	12	–	50: 115m, 119b
W v. Glos., Worc.	0	cw b M. Ball	3	4	–	–	
	79	b P. Bainbridge	60	45	8	3	50: 58m, 30b
W v. Som., Worc.	171*		292	280	29	1	50: 129m, 118b
							100: 207m, 182b
							150: 267m, 228b
	69*		132	103	9	–	50: 107m, 86b
W v. Glam., Abergavenny	252*		282	247	38	5	50: 64m, 54b
							100: 121m, 101b
							150: 189m, 158b
							200: 245m, 204b
							250: 282m, 247b
	100*		79	71	11	4	50: 42m, 40b
							100: 79m, 71b
W v. Derby, Derby	53	c A. Warner	112	103	8	–	50: 106m, 98b
W v. Kent, Canterbury	66	cw R. Ellison	134	108	10	–	50: 85m, 63b
	22	cw T. Wren	44	17	3	1	
W v. Leics, Le'ster	102	c J. Agnew	185	157	17	–	50: 104m, 85b
							100: 174m, 150b
	88*		125	105	8	2	50: 73m, 66b
W v. Lancs, Kidderm'r	67	c D. Hughes	121	112	8	1	50: 89m, 91b
W v. Hants, Worc.	72	cw L. Joseph	131	93	11	–	50: 93m, 63b
	50*		71	32	5	3	50: 71b, 32b
W v. N'hants, Worc.	34	cw N. Cook	62	69	3	–	
	50	st N. Cook	94	94	3	1	50: 93m, 92b
W v. Warks, Worc	14	cw G. Small	31	17	3	–	
	42	b D. Reeve	98	88	6	1	
W v. Notts, Trent B	4	cw F. Stephenson	12	8	1	–	
	18	c E. Hemmings	42	39	3	–	
W v. Glos., Bristol	110	c P. Bainbridge	233	229	13	–	50: 118m, 102b
							100: 223m, 212b
	38	c D. Graveney	70	62	7	–	
W v. Som., Taunton	154	c N. Mallender	231	195	27	1	50: 104m, 70b
							100: 183m, 138b
							150: 228m, 190b
	81	lbw A. Jones	84	88	11	2	50: 40m, 39b
W v. Glam., Worc.	6	cw S. Watkin	23	21	1	–	
	138*		185	155	18	1	50: 71m, 61b
							100: 151m, 133b

Runs for Hick's Teams

Runs for Worcestershire against each team

Against	Mch	Inn	N.o.	Runs	H.s.	Av'ge	100s	50s
Derbyshire	6	8	0	362	94	45.25	–	2
Essex	6	9	0	448	156	49.77	1	3
Glamorgan	10	16	4	1455	252*	121.25	7	2
Gloucestershire	10	16	1	871	138	58.06	4	3
Hampshire	6	10	1	466	177	51.77	1	3
Kent	6	8	0	435	147	54.37	1	2
Lancashire	9	15	1	521	212	37.21	2	1
Leicestershire	7	10	3	361	102	51.57	1	1
Middlesex	5	8	0	416	173	52.00	1	3
Northamptonshire	7	12	1	897	140*	81.54	5	3
Nottinghamshire	10	18	3	904	227*	60.26	1	8
Somerset	12	20	7	1693	405*	130.23	6	4
Surrey	7	10	1	572	127	63.55	2	3
Sussex	6	11	2	449	110*	49.88	3	–
Warwickshire	10	14	0	494	126	35.28	1	4
Yorkshire	4	6	1	515	198	103.00	2	2
Australians	1	2	0	56	43	28.00	–	–
Indians	1	1	0	70	70	–	–	1
New Zealanders	1	1	1	2	2*	–	–	–
Pakistanis	1	1	0	11	11	–	–	–
West Indians	1	1	0	172	172	–	1	–
MCC	2	2	1	245	173*	–	1	1
Oxford University	1	1	0	3	3	–	–	–
Total	129	200	27	11418	405*	65.58	40	46

Runs on each ground in first-class cricket in England

	Mch	Inn	N.o.	Runs	H.s.	Av'ge	100s	50s
Abergavenny	2	4	2	557	252*	278.50	3	–
Bournemouth	2	3	0	125	81	41.66	–	1
Bristol	5	9	0	473	121	52.55	2	2
Buxton	1	–	–	–	–	–	–	–
Canterbury	1	2	0	88	66	44.00	–	1
Cleethorpes	1	2	0	57	38	28.50	–	–
Colchester	2	2	0	228	156	114.00	1	1
Derby	3	4	0	225	94	56.25	–	2
Eastbourne	1	2	0	57	35	28.50	–	–
Edgbaston	6	10	0	409	126	40.90	1	4
Folkestone	1	1	0	21	21	–	–	–
Gloucester	1	2	0	162	138	81.00	1	–
Hove	2	4	1	214	110*	71.33	2	–
Leicester	3	4	2	227	102	113.50	1	1
Lord's	6	9	1	678	173*	84.75	2	4
Neath	2	4	1	312	219*	104.00	1	1
Northampton	3	5	0	345	111	69.00	2	1
Old Trafford	5	9	1	411	212	51.37	2	–
The Oval	6	7	1	380	127	63.33	1	2
Oxford	2	2	0	233	230	116.50	1	–
Pontypridd	1	–	–	–	–	–	–	–
Sheffield	2	2	0	204	150	102.00	1	1
Southend	1	2	0	80	51	40.00	–	1
Swansea	1	1	0	192	192	–	1	–
Taunton	4	5	1	678	405*	169.56	2	1
Trent Bridge	5	10	1	318	76	35.33	–	4
Tunbridge Wells	1	–	–	–	–	–	–	–
Weston-super-Mare	2	4	2	184	72	92.00	–	1
Kidderminster	4	5	1	191	67	47.75	–	2
Worcester	60	97	13	5065	227*	60.29	18	18
Total	136	211	27	12114	405*	65.83	42	48

Runs for Zimbabwean XIs against each team

Against	Mch	Inn	N.o.	Runs	H.s.	Av'ge	100s	50s
English Counties	2	4	0	85	42	21.25	–	–
Sri Lankan XI	2	3	0	70	57	23.33	–	1
Young Australia	2	3	0	288	154	96.00	2	–
Young India	2	4	0	64	23	16.00	–	–
Young New South Wales	1	2	0	44	40	22.00	–	–
Young New Zealand	4	8	1	304	95	43.42	–	2
Young West Indies	2	4	2	56	28 *	28.00	–	–
Glamorgan	1	1	0	192	192	–	1	–
Gloucestershire	1	2	0	40	39	20.00	–	–
Minor Counties XI	1	2	0	57	38	28.50	–	–
Oxford University	1	1	0	230	230	–	1	–
Surrey	1	1	0	10	10	–	–	–
Warwickshire	1	2	0	69	65	34.50	–	1
Total	21	37	3	1509	230	44.38	4	4

Runs on each ground in Zimbabwe

	Mch	Inn	N.o.	Runs	H.s.	Av'ge	100s	50s
Harare	12	23	3	811	154	40.55	2	2
Bulawayo	1	2	0	30	30	15.00	–	–
Total	13	25	3	841	154	38.22	2	2

Runs on each ground in Sri Lanka

	Mch	Inn	N.o.	Runs	H.s.	Av'ge	100s	50s
Colombo	1	2	0	66	57	33.00	–	1
Moratuwa	1	1	0	4	4	–	–	–
Total	2	3	0	70	57	23.33	–	1

Runs for Northern Districts against each team

	Mch	Inn	N.o.	Runs	H.s.	Av'ge	100s	50s
Auckland	4	7	1	493	211 *	82.16	2	–
Canterbury	3	6	1	412	145	82.40	2	1
Central Districts	3	4	0	251	105	62.75	1	2
Otago	3	5	1	272	122	68.00	1	1
Wellington	3	6	1	462	144	92.40	3	1
England XI	1	2	0	165	146	82.50	1	–
Total	17	30	4	2055	211 *	79.03	10	5

Runs on each ground in New Zealand

	Mch	Inn	N.o.	Runs	H.s.	Av'ge	100s	50s
Alexandra	1	2	0	94	90	47.00	–	1
Auckland	2	4	1	270	211 *	90.00	1	–
Christchurch	2	4	1	196	113 *	65.33	1	–
Gisborne	1	2	1	56	44 *	–	–	–
Hamilton	6	10,	0	790	146	79.00	4	2
Morrinsville	1	2	0	276	144	138.00	2	–
Napier	1	2	0	162	105	81.00	1	1
Palmerston North	1	1	0	62	62	–	–	1
Te Awamutu	1	1	0	27	27	–	–	–
Wellington	1	2	1	122	121 *	–	1	–
Total	17	30	4	2055	211 *	79.03	10	5

Century stands involving Graeme Hick

Season	Runs	Wkt	Hick's Score	Partner & Score	Match
1984	133*	8	82*	P.A. Neale 72*	Worcs v. Surrey, The Oval
1985	277	4	230	D.L. Houghton 104	Zimb. v. Oxford U, Oxford
	148	2	192	G.A. Paterson 69	Zimb. v. Glamorgan, Swansea
	101	6	56	P.A. Neale 62	Worcs v. Essex, Worcester
	108	4	62	P.A. Neale 92*	Worcs v. Warks, Edgbaston
	135	2	174*	T.S. Curtis 58	Worcs v. Somerset, Worcester
	117	2	128	T.S. Curtis 55	Worcs v. N'hants, Worcester
1986	100	3	62	D.M. Smith 102	Worcs v. Warks, Edgbaston
	138	4	227*	P.A. Neale 57	Worcs v. Notts, Worcester
	287*	2	219*	T.S. Curtis 66*	Worcs v. Glamorgan, Neath
	108	3	81	D.B. D'Oliveira 26	Worcs v. Hants, Bournemouth
	157	3	85	D.B. D'Oliveira 146*	Worcs v. Glos., Bristol
	128	3	107	P.A. Neale 60*	Worcs v. Glamorgan, Worcester
1987	154	2	107	M.J. Weston 52	Worcs v. Sussex, Worcester
	231	2	138	T.S. Curtis 91	Worcs v. Glos., Glo'ster
	100	2	63	T.S. Curtis 110	Worcs v. Notts, Kidderminster
	151	4	132	P.A. Neale 103*	Worcs v. Somerset, Worcester
	258	2	173	T.S Curtis 129	Worcs v. Middlesex, Lord's
	125	2	126	G.J. Lord 36	Worcs v. Warks, Edgbaston
	130	3	126	T.S. Curtis 94	Worcs v. Warks, Edgbaston
	134	2	156	T.S. Curtis 44	Worcs v. Essex, Colchester
	102	4	156	P.A. Neale 100*	Worcs v. Essex, Colchester
1987/8	117	2	64	L.M. Crocker 99	ND v. Wellington, Hamilton
	144*	3	113*	D.J. White 33*	ND v. Canterbury, Christchurch
	188	3	146	D.J. White 80	ND v. England XI, Hamilton
	198	4	122	B.G. Cooper 88	ND v. Otago, Hamilton
	170	3	141	D.J. White 77	ND v. Auckland, Hamilton
1988	202	4	212	P.A. Neale 40	Worcs v. Lancs, Old Trafford
	112	2	86	T.S. Curtis 34	Worcs v. Notts, Worcester
	265	6	405*	S.J. Rhodes 56	Worcs v. Somerset, Taunton
	177*	8	405*	R.K. Illingworth 31*	Worcs v. Somerset, Taunton
	284	2	172	T.S. Curtis 82	Worcs v. West Indians, Worcester
	110	2	78	T.S. Curtis 108	Worcs v. Middlesex, Lord's
	276	2	177	T.S. Curtis 131	Worcs v. Hants, Worcester
	205	7	198	P.J. Newport 77*	Worcs v. Yorks, Worcester
	139	4	132	P.A. Neale 44	Worcs v. N'hants, Worcester
	192	2	159	T.S. Curtis 86	Worcs v. Glamorgan, Abergavenny
	117	4	159	P.A. Neale 51	Worcs v. Glamorgan, Abergavenny
	127	4	127	P.A. Neale 35	Worcs v. Surrey, The Oval
	112	2	121	G.J. Lord 41	Worcs v. Glos., Bristol
	143	4	197	P.A. Neale 29	Worcs v. Glamorgan, Worcester
1988/9	117	3	57	D.J. White 77	ND v. C Dists, Napier
	182	2	105	D.J. White 73	ND v. C Dists, Napier
	136	8	121*	S.A. Thomson 65	ND v. Wellington, Wellington
	103	3	145	D.J. White 37	ND v. Canterbury, Hamilton
	136	4	145	C.M. Kuggeleijn 101*	ND v. Canterbury, Hamilton
	103	3	71	D.J. White 110	ND v. Canterbury, Hamilton
	104	4	221*	C.M. Kuggeleijn 33	ND v. Auckland, Auckland
	146*	6	221*	S.A. Thomson 31*	ND v. Auckland, Auckland
	118	3	144	D.J. White 37	ND v. Wellington, Morrinsville
1989	105	3	173*	G.J. Lord 80	Worcs v. MCC, Lord's
	126*	4	90*	P.A. Neale 51*	Worcs v. Notts, Worcester
	108	3	150	T.S. Curtis 43	Worcs v. Yorks, Sheffield

Season	Runs	Wkt	Hick's Score	Partner & Score	Match
	107	4	150	D.B. D'Oliveira 30	Worcs v. Yorks, Sheffield
	112	5	111	P.A. Neale 62	Worcs v. N'hants, No'ton
	144	3	110*	D.B. D'Oliveira 55	Worcs v. Sussex, Hove
	135	2	147	P. Bent 144	Worcs v. Kent, Worcester
	113	3	72	T.S. Curtis 156	Worcs v. Essex, Colchester
	153	3	86	D.B. D'Oliveira 63	Worcs v. Somerset, Worcester
	128	2	136*	T.S. Curtis 84	Worcs v. Somerset, Worcester
1990	117*	3	106*	I.T. Botham 50*	Worcs v. Lancs, Old Trafford
	109	2	97	T.S. Curtis 46	Worcs v. Notts, Worcester
	123	4	80	D.B. D'Oliveira 87*	Worcs v. Middlesex, Lord's
	139	3	171*	D.B. D'Oliveira 55	Worcs v. Somerset, Worcester
	148*	4	171*	P.A. Neale 49*	Worcs v. Somerset, Worcester
	175*	2	100*	T.S. Curtis 111*	Worcs v. Glamorgan, Abergavenny
	104	2	252*	P. Bent 69	Worcs v. Glamorgan, Abergavenny
	264	3	252*	D.B. D'Oliveira 121	Worcs v. Glamorgan, Abergavenny
	193	2	102	T.S. Curtis 151*	Worcs v. Leics, Leicester
	164	2	72	G.J. Lord 190	Worcs v. Hants, Worcester
	105	2	110	T.S. Curtis 96	Worcs v. Glos., Bristol
	263	2	154	T.S. Curtis 156	Worcs v. Somerset, Taunton
	138	2	81	G.J. Lord 80	Worcs v. Somerset, Taunton
	117	2	138*	T.S. Curtis 60	Worcs v. Glamorgan, Worcester

Partnership records for Worcs held by Hick

Wicket	Runs	Partners	Match
2	287*	G.A. Hick & T.S. Curtis	v. Glamorgan, Neath 1986
6	265	G.A. Hick & S.J. Rhodes	v. Somerset, Taunton 1988
7	205	G.A. Hick & T.J. Newport	v. Yorks, Worcester 1988
8	177*	G.A. Hick & R.K. Illingworth	v. Somerset, Taunton 1988

Partnership record for Northern Districts held by Hick

Wicket	Runs	Partners	Match
4	187	G.A. Hick & B.G. Cooper	v. Otago, Hamilton 1987/8

Hick's record in all types of cricket

John Hick, Graeme's father, calculates that his son had scored twenty-three centuries in all forms of cricket before he arrived at Worcester in April 1984. His hundredth century overall came on 15 January 1989 when he scored 121 not out for Northern Districts at Wellington in a Shell Trophy match. It was his thirty-sixth hundred in first-class cricket. Graeme Hick was twenty-two years and six months old at the time. Mr Hick calculates that Graeme had scored 124 hundreds in all competitive cricket at the end of the 1990 English season.

Some first-class career milestones
■ Graeme Hick's first recording of 2000 runs in a season – 1986 – saw him become the youngest batsman ever to perform this feat. The leaders are as follows:

Age (Yrs-days)	Runs	Av'ge	Season	Player
20–111	2004	64.64	1986	G.A. Hick
21–33	2888	56.62	1937	L. Hutton
21–65	2468	56.09	1939	D.C.S. Compton
21–163	2154	44.87	1937	W.J. Edrich

Hick's 2000 runs in 1988 put him ninth on the list.

With the Northern Districts
■ Hick spent 1987/8 and 1988/9 playing for the New Zealand team, Northern Districts, and made seventeen appearances in all. Hick's 2055 runs, average 79.03, place him twelfth on the all-time list of run-getters for Northern Districts and his ten centuries put him top of the list. His seasons' aggregates of 1238 runs in 1988/9 and 827 runs in 1987/8 are the best two for a season, while his 211* in 1988/9 is the highest score for Northern Districts.

■ During April 1988 Hick scored 410 first-class runs for an average of 82.00. This set a new record for April in England, beating the previous record of D.L. Amiss in 1976 by 3 runs.

■ At the end of May 1988 Hick's 172 against the West Indians at Worcester saw him reach 1000 runs for the season. The other batsmen to perform this feat before the end of May are:

1895	W.G. Grace	1016 runs	(112.88)
1900	T.W. Hayward	1074 runs	(97.63)
1927	W.R. Hammond	1042 runs	(74.42)
1928	C. Hallows	1000 runs	(125.00)
1930	D.G. Bradman	1001 runs	(143.00)
1938	D.G. Bradman	1056 runs	(150.85)
1938	W.J. Edrich	1010 runs	(84.16)
1973	G.M. Turner	1018 runs	(78.30)
1988	G.A. Hick	1019 runs	(101.90)

■ Hick required eleven innings to pass four figures for the season; this puts him high on the list of quick scorers of 1000 runs, by innings:

1938	D.G. Bradman	7 inns
1895	W.G. Grace	10 inns
1948	D.G. Bradman	10 inns
1988	G.A. Gooch	10 inns
1928	C. Hallows	11 inns
1930	D.G. Bradman	11 inns
1971	G. Boycott	11 inns
1988	G.A. Hick	11 inns

With Worcestershire

■ Graeme Hick's epic 405 not out for Worcestershire against Somerset at Taunton in May 1988 naturally contained a number of statistical highlights.

It was the highest score made in a first-class match in England since A.C. MacLaren's 424 made for Lancashire, also against Somerset at Taunton, in 1895. For Worcestershire it beat the previous record of 311 not out by Glenn Turner against Warwickshire at Worcester in 1982.

Hick's score created a new record for a batsman in May, beating the 357 by R. Abel for Surrey against Somerset at Taunton in 1899. He also set a new record in English first-class cricket for a batsman going in no. 3 in the order; the previous best was 345 by C.G. Macartney for the Australians against Nottinghamshire at Trent Bridge in 1921.

The second-highest scorer for Worcestershire was Stephen Rhodes with 56. The disparity between the two top scores of 349 runs is the largest ever for one innings in English first-class cricket. In world cricket it is beaten by the two following cases;

396: Hanif Mohammed (499), Wallis Mathias (103), Karachi v. Bahawalpur, Karachi 1958/9
356: B. Sutcliffe (385), A.W. Gilbertson (29), Otago v. Canterbury, Christchurch 1952/3

Hick set two Worcestershire partnership records during his innings:

265 for 6th wicket with S.J. Rhodes
177 for 8th wicket (unbroken) with R.K. Illingworth.

■ In 1988 Hick scored 1169 runs, average 73.06, at Worcester: only Glenn Turner with 1236, average 77.25, in 1970 has exceeded this season's aggregate. Hick also scored 1028 runs, average 68.53, at Worcester in 1986.

■ During the 1990 season Hick had a run of 645 runs before being dismissed. After scoring 171 not out and 69 not out against Somerset at Worcester, he went on to Abergavenny where he scored 252 not out and 100 not out. He was finally dismissed, for 53, in the following match, against Derbyshire at Derby. Hick's run was a record for English first-class cricket but he narrowly failed to beat the world record, as the table shows.

Runs before dismissal	Batsman	Scores	Where played	Season
709	K.C. Ibrahim	218* 36* 234* 77* 144	India	1947/8
645	G.A. Hick	171* 69* 252* 100* 53	England	1990
634	V. Merchant	170* 243* 221	India	1941/2
630	E.H. Hendren	205* 254* 171	West Indies	1929/30
575	E.D. Weekes	246* 200* 129	England	1950
558	F. Jakeman	80* 258* 176* 44	England	1951

Appendices

■ During his innings of 252 not out for Worcestershire against Glamorgan at Abergavenny in 1990 – a match which saw 1641 runs scored, a record for a non-Test match in England – Hick completed 10,000 runs in first-class county cricket. In passing this milestone Hick achieved at least four new records, the details of which follow:

10,000 runs for a county in fewest innings: top two

Player (county)	Match & season in which achieved	Innings taken
Graeme Hick (Worcs)	Worcs v. Glam., Abergavenny 1990	179
K.S. Ranjitsinjhi (Sussex)	Sussex v. Glos., Bristol 1899	187

10,000 runs for a county at youngest age: top two

Player (county)	Match & season in which achieved	Age
Graeme Hick (Worcs)	Worcs v. Glam., Abergavenny 1990	24 yrs 59 days
W.R. Hammond (Glos)	Glos in 1929	25 yrs

10,000 runs for Worcestershire in fewest innings: top two

Player	Match & season in which achieved	Innings taken
Graeme Hick	Worcs v. Glam., Abergavenny 1990	179
Glenn Turner	Worcs v. Warks, Worcester 1975	240

10,000 runs for Worcestershire at youngest age: top two

Player	Match & season in which achieved	Age
Graeme Hick	Worcs v. Glam., Abergavenny 1990	24 yrs 59 days
Ron Headley	Worcs v. Leics, Leicester 1966	27 yrs

Other Records

■ In the second innings of the match with Glamorgan in 1990 (see above) Hick scored 100* to become the youngest batsman ever to obtain fifty first-class centuries. Hick was 24 years and 61 days, whereas Sir Donald Bradman, the previous holder of this record, had been 26.

Hick was unable to overtake Bradman with regard to innings taken, however; Bradman completed his fifty centuries in 175 innings whereas Hick required 249 innings. Hick is well ahead of the third player on the list, W.G. Grace with 275 innings.

At the end of the 1990 season Hick had scored fifty-four centuries in 269 innings, an average of a century for every 4.98 innings. For batsmen with fifty centuries or more Hick was in second place with regard to century rate. The leaders were:

Player	Centuries	Innings	Inns per 100
D.G. Bradman	117	338	2.89
G.A. Hick	54	269	4.98
A.L. Hassett	59	322	5.46
W.R. Hammond	167	1005	6.02

■ Among batsmen with fewer than fifty centuries, G.A. Headley averaged 4.97 innings for each of his thirty-three hundreds, while W.M. Woodfull and W.H. Ponsford scored forty-nine and forty-seven centuries respectively at one every 5 innings.

■ Graeme Hick finished the 1990 season with a career record of 15,080 runs for an average of 64.17, with fifty-four centuries, and one felt it would be interesting to compare this career record with that of other leading batsmen at the end of the season when they had reached 15,000 runs. Obviously it would be impractical to examine *all* batsmen so I restricted the project to those who had exceeded 100 centuries in their whole career. It will be seen from the table below that with the exception of the unapproachable Bradman – and would he have maintained such amazing form had he played as much as the others – Hick's record at this specific stage is superior to all.

I have listed all those players who averaged more than 47; such players as Hobbs do not qualify. At the end of the 1911 season his record was 15,741 runs, thirty-four centuries. 38.11 average, his age was twenty-eight. At his retirement of course Hobbs had expanded his record to 61,167 runs, 197 hundreds, 50.68 average. Without suggesting such a happening is at all likely, at his present rate Hick will pass Hobb's record number of runs in his 1092nd first-class innings, when his average will stand at 64.11. By then he will have scored 218 centuries, having passed Hobbs' present record of 197 in his 990th innings. Unfortunately at his career rate to date of 38 innings per year Hick will be about forty-five years old when he exceeds Hobbs' runs record and forty-three when he passes his centuries total. All speculation of course; Hick may retire early, or lose his form, but my projections are based on his performances throughout his whole career to date. *Almost* without exception all those players who have exceeded 100 centuries improved their average runs per innings and rate of century scoring after they had passed a career total of 15,000 runs and fifty centuries, so it is statistically probable that given normal luck and health Hick will pass Hobbs in his early forties!

Other Interesting Facts

Career records after 15,000+ runs of Leading players with 100 centuries

Player	Runs	100s	Av'ge	Age
D.G. Bradman	15,033	53	92.79	28
G.A. Hick	15,080	54	64.17	24
D.C.S. Compton	16,505	57	59.15	29
W.G. Grace	16,647	57	56.62	28
L. Hutton	15,259	45	50.52	30
Zaheer Abbas	15,835	49	50.11	29
I.V.A. Richards	16,082	45	48.00	28
W.R. Hammond	16,038	48	47.87	26

Hick's Mode of dismissal

Season	Bld	ct wt	ct fld	lbw	st	ro
1983/4	4	2	1	–	1	1
1984	–	–	–	–	–	–
1984/5	–	2	4	3	1	1
1985	11	2	10	1	–	–

Season	Bld	ct wt	ct fld	lbw	st	ro
1985/6	–	1	3	1	–	–
1986	6	8	14	1	1	1
1987	5	6	14	9	2	–
1987/8	4	–	8	1	–	–
1988	9	7	16	3	–	–
1988/9	4	3	6	–	–	–
1989	7	3	14	8	–	–
1990	5	10	9	1	1	–
Total	53	44	99	28	6	3

In an effort to try and pinpoint any weaknesses (relatively speaking!) I listed, season by season, Hick's modes of dismissal, as above. Without claiming anything for the figures other than curiosity value, it does appear that Hick sometimes has periods when he forgets where the stumps are in relation to his legs and, as one might expect, he is frequently caught at the wicket off his 'favourite' slash.

Most successful bowlers against Hick

In an attempt to find any weaknesses Hick may have shown against specific bowlers I analysed all his dismissals but as with 'Modes of dismissal' the results were far from conclusive.

Hick has been dismissed on five occasions by Nick Cook, a left-armed spinner now of Northants, previously of Leicestershire and winner of fifteen England caps during the 1980s, and by Adrian Jones, a well-built right-armed pace bowler with spirit but no great subtlety, now of Somerset, formerly of Sussex. David Graveney, Gloucestershire left-arm spinner, has dismissed Hick four times, so too have Tim Munton, Warwickshire seamer relying on control and accuracy rather than pace, and Neil Foster of Essex and England and a slightly more fiery individual.

The lack of a pattern is manifest; one concludes that Hick is nobody's rabbit, and for the most part it is a lottery as to who will get him out!

Hick in Limited-overs cricket

For Zimbabwean team

	Mch	Inn.	N.o.	Runs.	Hs.	Av'ge
1982/3 ZC/YZ/CD	3	3	0	3	2	1.00
1983 Zimb. in Eng	6	4	0	61	52	15.25
1983/4 Zimb. sides	15	14	2	228	62*	19.00
1984/5 Zimb./CD	11	11	1	310	61*	31.00
1985 Zimb.	6	6	0	233	75	38.83
1985/6 Zimb.	10	10	0	153	77	15.30
Total	51	48	3	988	77	21.95

Note:
ZC = Zimbabwe Colts; YZ = Young Zimbabwe; CD = Country Districts.

For Northern Districts in Shell Cup

	Mch	Inn.	N.o.	Runs.	Hs.	Av'ge	Ct	Overs	Mdns	Runs	Wts	Av'ge
1987/8	5	5	0	154	100	30.80	4	42.5	7	142	6	23.66
1988/9	5	5	0	122	42	24.40	1					
Total	10	10	0	276	100	27.60	1	42.5	7	142	6	23.66

Appendices

Limited-overs cricket in England

Season	Inn.	N.o.	Runs	H.s.	Av'ge	Ct	Overs	Mdns	Runs	Wts	Av'ge
Nat-West Trophy											
1986	4	1	37	27	12.33	3	10	1	25	1	
1987	2	1	227	172 *	–	1					
1988	5	0	296	138	59.20	3	41.3	3	133	8	16.62
1989	4	2	228	90 *	114.00	1	15	0	67	0	
1990	3	1	129	78 *	64.50	–	24	2	69	0	
Total	18	5	917	172 *	70.53	8	90.3	6	294	9	32.66

Season	Inn.	N.o.	Runs	H.s.	Av'ge	Ct	Overs	Mdns	Runs	Wts	Av'ge
Benson & Hedges Cup											
1986	6	2	345	103 *	86.25	4	12	1	47	3	15.66
1987	5	1	265	88	66.25	2	8	0	30	0	
1988	4	0	87	47	21.75	3	3	0	8	0	
1989	4	0	170	109	42.50	3	10	0	50	0	
1990	6	1	165	64	33.00	5	30	0	125	4	31.25
Total	25	4	1032	109	49.14	17	63	1	260	7	37.14
Sunday League											
1985	8	1	205	90	29.28	3	10	0	66	3	22.00
1986	16	1	507	68 *	33.80	2	14	0	70	2	35.00
1987	16	6	599	88	59.90	5	69.1	1	334	10	33.40
1988	14	2	512	111	42.66	1	20	0	132	6	22.00
1989	15	1	435	84	31.07	2	36	0	197	6	32.83
1990	13	3	751	114 *	75.10	4	31.5	1	200	6	33.33
Total	82	14	3009	114 *	44.25	17	181	2	999	33	30.27
Refuge Assurance											
1988	2	1	76	74 *	–	–					
1989	1	0	0	0 –	–						
Total	3	1	76	74 *	38.00	–					

Picture Acknowledgements

Allsport/Simon Bruty: page 2 above and below
Allsport/Adrian Murrell: page 6
Allsport/Ben Radford: page 8
Patrick Eagar: pages 1 and 7
Les Jacques: page 5 above and below
Ken Kelly: page 4 below